GUITAR *SCHOOL*

**TRANSCRIBED SOLOS AND
EXCERPTS COMPLETE
WITH LESSONS**

BY JESSE GRESS

THE BEATLES GUITAR TECHNIQUES

ISBN 0-7935-0249-7

HAL•LEONARD™
CORPORATION
7777 W. BLUEMOUND RD. P.O. BOX 13819 MILWAUKEE, WI 53213

THE BEATLES
GUITAR TECHNIQUES

CONTENTS

INTRODUCTION

In their heyday, the Beatles made music that was highly contagious, affecting millions of people and undoubtedly inspiring many of them to pick up a guitar for the first time. John Lennon, George Harrison and Paul McCartney popularized electric and acoustic guitars to an extent that made the instrument practically irresistible. Unfortunately, no printed music existed that provided accurately notated guitar parts. Piano/vocal arrangements were the norm and never seemed to get it right in the guitar department. In retrospect, it's not too hard to understand why. The way the Beatles used guitars was far from "normal," and the guitars alone were often only a portion of the complete musical picture. As guitarists, John, George and Paul were pioneers of a brave new world devoid of the high-tech electronic arsenal available today. Besides basic amp distortion and fuzztones, effects were generated either at the mixing console (compression, echo and equalization) or the tape machine (flanging, delay and automated double-tracking, or ADT). The Beatles' "guitarsenal" included 6 and 12-string electrics and acoustics, nylon string acoustics and a few small amplifiers. Favored brands were Gretsch, Rickenbacker, Gibson, Epiphone, Fender and Vox.

Beginning with solid folk, rock 'n' roll, and rockabilly backgrounds, the Beatles took the guitar on an evolutionary journey from 1963 to 1970 that defined an entire vocabulary of guitar styles, sounds and textures. Early on, signature guitar riffs became instrumental hooks as often as their vocal melodies. John, George and Paul were all talented soloists and accompanists, each with a distinct style. Producer George Martin's influence may be heard especially in the post-Revolver era as the guitar parts became more orchestrated. But however much they evolved, the Beatles never seemed to drastically change styles, only to merge the new with the old. Their earliest folk influences were still evident on many of their last recordings.

This book presents a guided tour, designed to take the magic and mystery out of the many roles the guitar has played throughout the Beatles' career. The song excerpts are presented chronologically in order of release in the U.K., which corresponds to the current U.S. CD releases. Highlights are discussed in the text preceding each transcription. Every effort has been made to label who played which part, and measure numbers and minute/second indicators are used to pinpoint the starting and stopping points of each excerpt throughout. Though this music was recorded between 20 and 30 years ago, it maintains its freshness to date, and putting it under the microscope can help explain why. There's an embarrassment of riches presented in the following pages for both the novice and the professional. So, roll up! You've got an invitation!

Jesse Gress 2/13/92

PLEASE PLEASE ME

From the album *Please Please Me*
Words and Music by John Lennon and Paul McCartney

Though John Lennon's harmonica intro was featured on the recorded version of the Beatles' first single, George Harrison had no problem covering the part live. He may be seen playing octaves on the 1st and 4th strings with his pick and middle finger during a performance on the Ed Sullivan show released on video as "The Beatles' First U.S. Visit." The simple rhythmic strumming pattern provides an effective accompaniment to the pedal-point harmonized vocal melody. The occasional percussive 16th note flourishes add excitement as does the low-register guitar break leading to the chorus. It was this kind of signature riff that grabbed the public ear. The band went on to exploit this concept to the hilt, and melodic vocal phrases answered by recognizable guitar figures soon became a Beatles trademark.

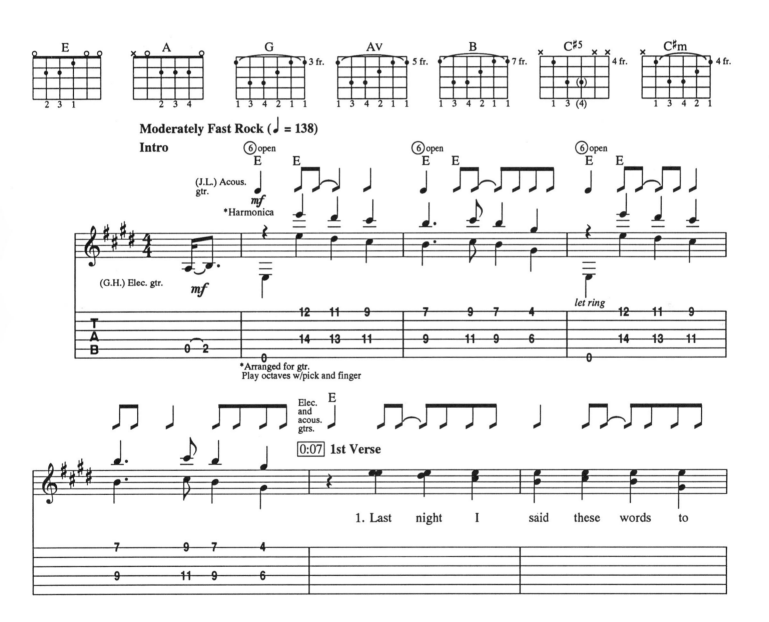

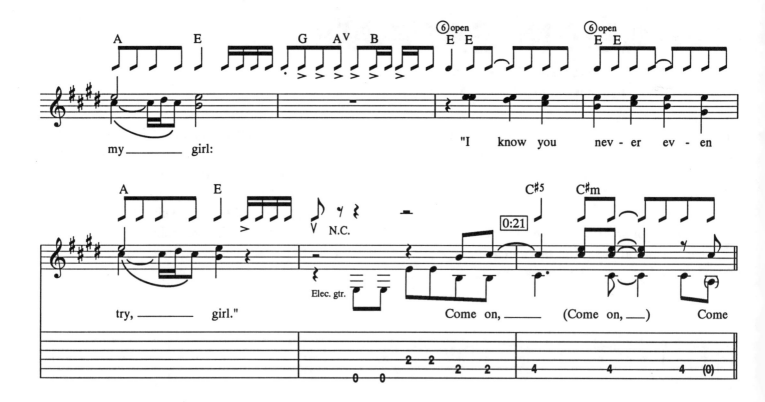

LOVE ME DO

From the album *Past Masters I, Please Please Me*
Words and Music by John Lennon and Paul McCartney

Another harmonica intro (a staple in early Beatles material) kicked off the Beatles' first single, this time over a swing-8th rhythm figure using two simple chords. Note the common tone (G) on top of both the G and C chords and the alternating bass note/chord strum pattern. The two-bar figure accents beats "2" and "4" of the first measure and "2-and" as well as "4" on the second.

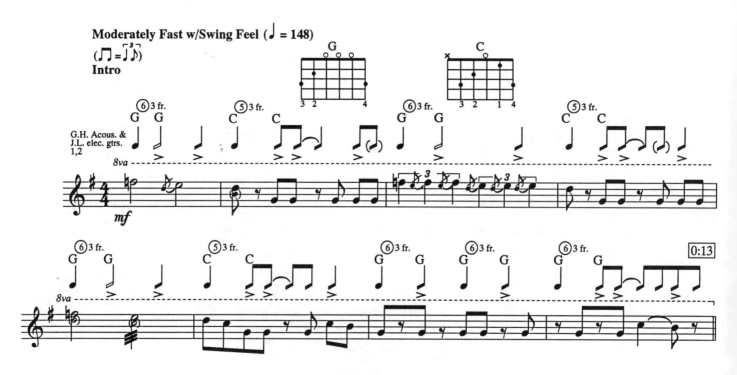

TWIST AND SHOUT

From the album *Please Please Me*
Words and Music by Bert Russell and Phil Medley

George's 8-bar "Twist and Shout" solo is played using partial chord forms. The bottom three notes of a 2nd position D barre chord move to a partial 3rd position G, then back to open A before setting up the repeat with a partial G to D. The 6-bar V chord rave-up leads back to the verse.

FROM ME TO YOU

From the album *Past Masters I*

Words and Music by John Lennon and Paul McCartney

Once again, a signature harmonica and guitar provide an intro that would later be played entirely on guitar when performed live. A greater sense of interplay between rhythm guitar parts had developed; George's staccato chords bounced nicely off of John's jangly strumming.

*Harmonica arr. for guitar.
Play octaves w/pick and finger.

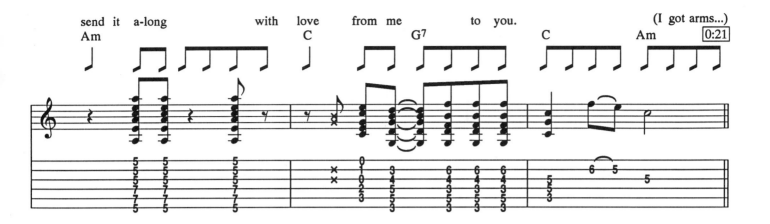

SHE LOVES YOU

From the album *Past Masters I*
Words and Music by John Lennon and Paul McCartney

George's double-stop fills harmonized in 4ths punctuate this example. The rhythm guitar figure features a common phenomenon found throughout the Beatle's (and many other's) repetoire. Often, the top four (or so) open strings are used as an all-purpose passing chord (G⁶) in order to buy time to make a smooth, clean chord change. This usually occurs unconsciously on the "and" of beats 2 or 4 during an 8th or 16th note-based rhythm. Another variation of this is to change the entire chord a half beat early. At B, the guitars split into two distinct parts, with George playing full, sustained chords over John's rhythmic strumming. Particularly noteworthy is George's trebly, compressed G, Gmaj⁷ to G⁶ chord fill and subsequent return to the verse via the previously heard double-stop lick.

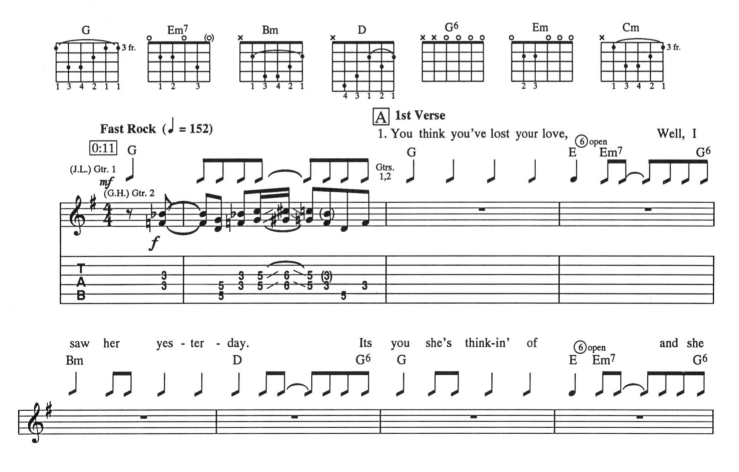

10

IT WON'T BE LONG

From the album _With The Beatles_
Words and Music by John Lennon and Paul McCartney

It's possible to get a lot of musical mileage by playing off of different parts of a barre or open chord shape. This rhythm figure features alternations between the lower and upper registers of various chord shapes and is structured more loosely than a single-note alternating bass pattern.

The tune begins with an 8-bar chorus before moving to a 7-bar verse figure punctuated by another twangy riff from George. The Beatles were masters at creating natural sounding melodies featuring odd numbers of measures. Here, a 2-bar melody is stated then answered by a 1-bar guitar fill. This repeats, with the guitar fill being played twice as a lead into the chorus. The open G^6 passing chord is also evident throughout the verse.

ALL MY LOVING

From the album *With The Beatles*
Words and Music by John Lennon and Paul McCartney

A brisk, swinging 8th note feel sets the pace for a great tune featuring great parts. John relentlessly strums 4 note voicings in triplets while George accents beats "2-and" and "4" underneath. You can really appreciate that open G6 passing chord after attempting to play John's part! The chord progression moves through the ii, V, I, vi, IV, ii, ♭VII and V chords in the key of E.

All My Loving (Solo)

George's solo opens with a snapped ascending bass line; he can be seen fretting with his thumb on an Ed Sullivan appearance. He creates a Chet Atkins-style sound by using 6ths and 5ths built from chord forms over John Lennon's bass/chord rhythm figure. The solo is wrapped up with an open position hammered triplet lick. Don't forget to swing it!

15

TILL THERE WAS YOU

From the album *With The Beatles*

By Meredith Willson

A cha-cha rhythm figure provides the backing for what sounds like a very composed pick-style nylon-string solo from George. He combines scale lines, arpeggios, and chord melody-style lines into a remarkably sophisticated solo that is worth scrutinizing. This is one of several Beatle tunes featuring a Latin flavor.

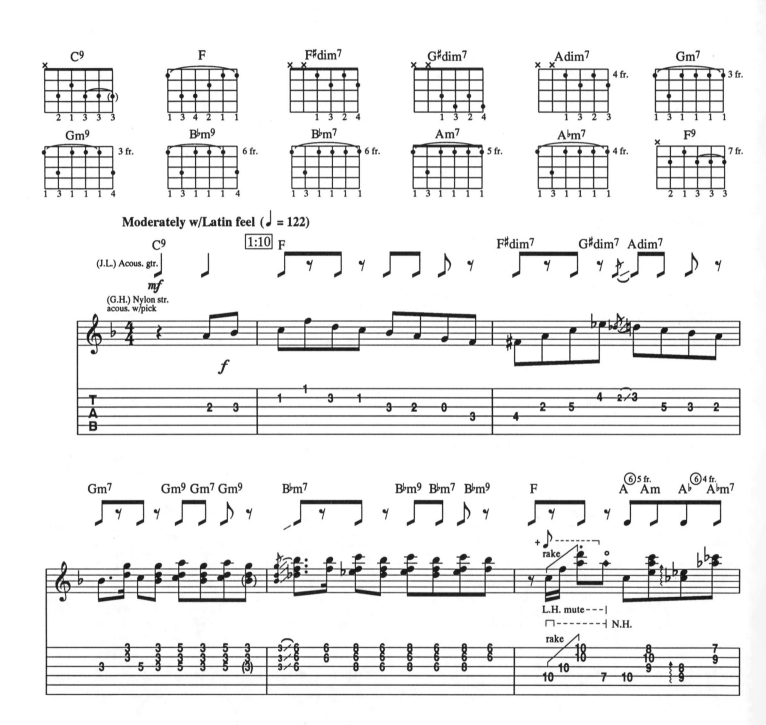

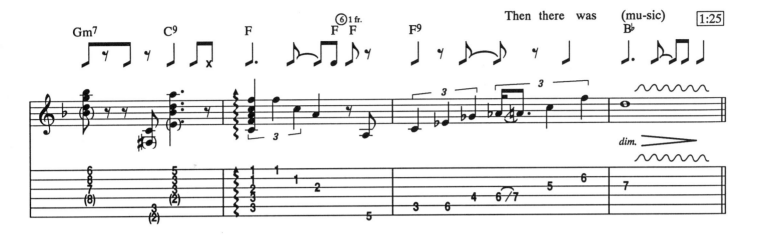

HOLD ME TIGHT

From the album *With The Beatles*
Words and Music by John Lennon and Paul McCartney

This rhythm figure is built on an ascending "walking" bass figure that figured prominently in much of the Beatles' music. The basic line plays the root twice, followed by the ♭3rd, the ♮3rd, the 5th played twice, the 6th and a return to the 5th. This pattern is moved through the I, IV, II and V chords in the key of F with variations throughout.

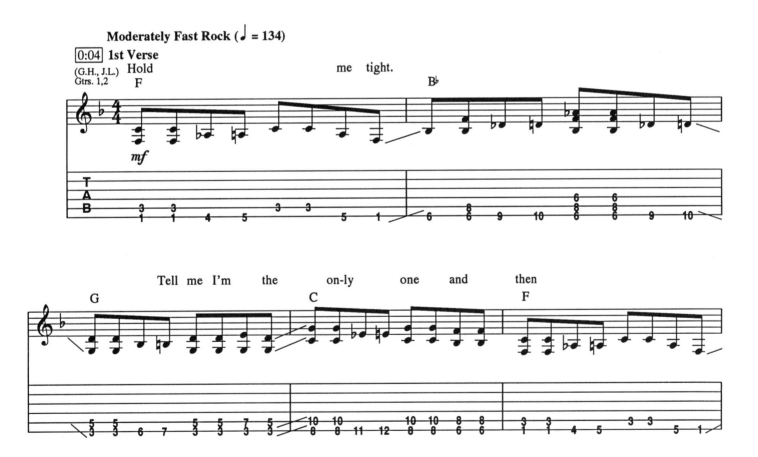

I might   nev-er be   the   lone-ly one,   so

I WANT TO HOLD YOUR HAND

From the album *Past Masters I*

Words and Music by John Lennon and Paul McCartney

The Beatles' first U.S. top-40 hit, which maintained the No. 1 chart position for seven weeks, was a 50/50 Lennon/McCartney collaboration. The intro features John playing a IV to V chord (C to D) rhythm figure while George plays mostly single-note fills. Chuck Berry's influence is evident in the alternating root/5 to root/6 chords used through the 12-bar verse progression, but the resemblance ends there. The I(G), V(D), vi(E5 or Em), and III^7(B^7) chords gave the 12-bar form a previously unheard twist.

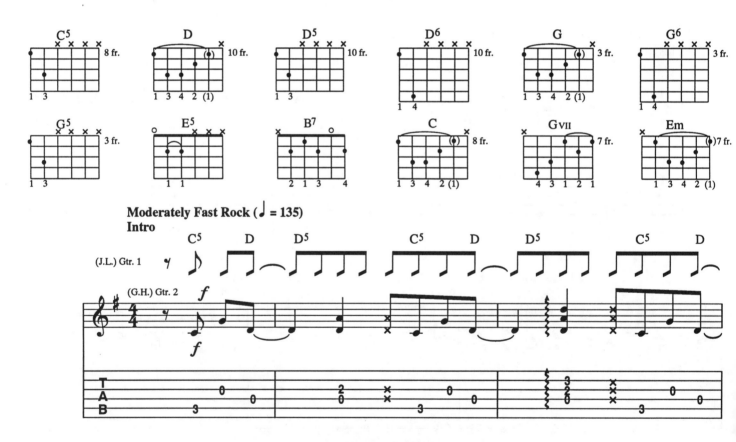

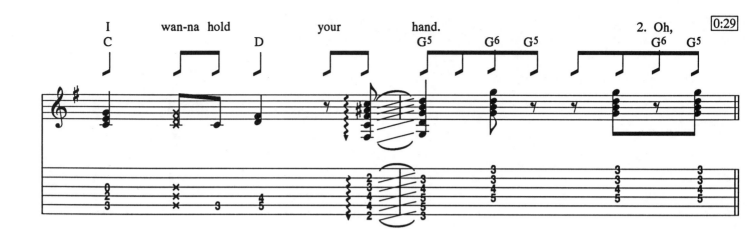

THIS BOY (RINGO'S THEME)

From the album *Past Masters I*

Words and Music by John Lennon and Paul McCartney

This Motown-style ballad employs a somewhat busy 12/8 rhythm pattern consisting of a standard I, vi, ii, V progression. Note George's use of left-hand muting, which selectively allows certain beats to ring out and others to be cut short. In this excerpt, play the chords notated with a staccato symbol (a dot above or below the notehead) with a quick but slight release of left hand (or fretting hand for you southpaws) pressure.

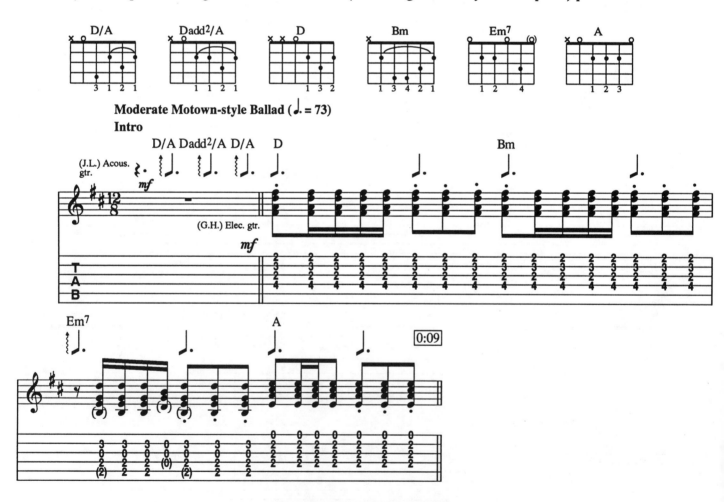

MCA music publishing

I CALL YOUR NAME

From the album *Past Masters I*
Words and Music by John Lennon and Paul McCartney

George's electric 12-string lines throughout the bridge create a "walking" bass figure similar to the one used in "Hold Me Tight." The main difference here is how the line moves through the chord progression. (IV - A, vi - C#m, II - F#7, #V - C7, V - B7). Notice how George adapts the basic line to fit over C#m by using the 2nd and ♭3rd instead of the ♭3 to the ♮3rd. John's rhythm part provides another example of his alternate bass/treble register chord-form strumming. The part also features some nice syncopations, as well as tasty #9 altered extensions on the #V and V chords.

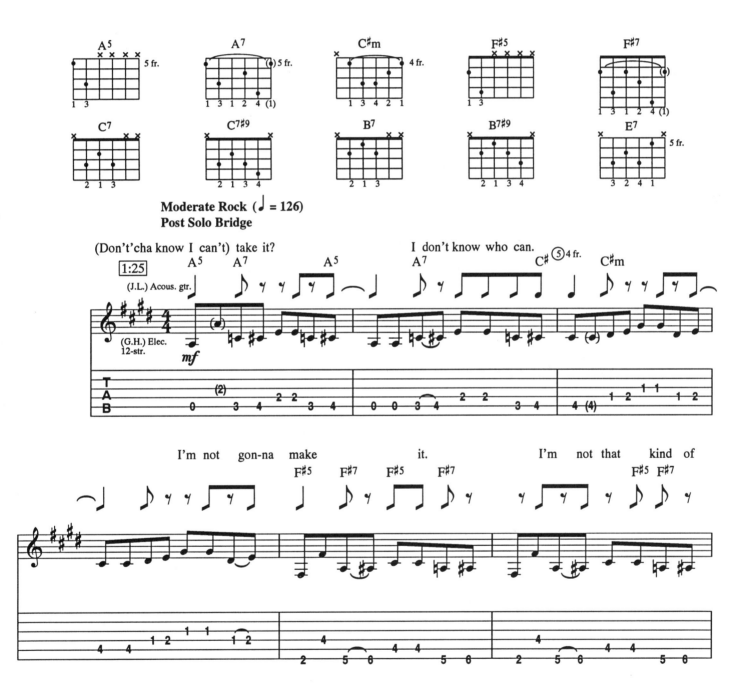

I SHOULD HAVE KNOWN BETTER

From the album *Hard Day's Night*

Words and Music by John Lennon and Paul McCartney

This 12-string electric solo begins with George quoting the vocal melody with a few added syncopations. Beginning at bar 6, the melody is harmonized in 3rds before coming to rest on an Em triad, which functions as a hip G^6 voicing over the G bass note and rhythm guitar chord. This use of single notes to doublestops to a triad effectively thickens the texture over the course of the solo, but in an extremely subtle way. The entire progression spans 10 bars but feels as natural as any standard 8, 12, or 16 bar progression. Rhythmically, John's acoustic playing is similar to his part behind the "I Call Your Name" solo; however, in this case, the chords are allowed to ring out.

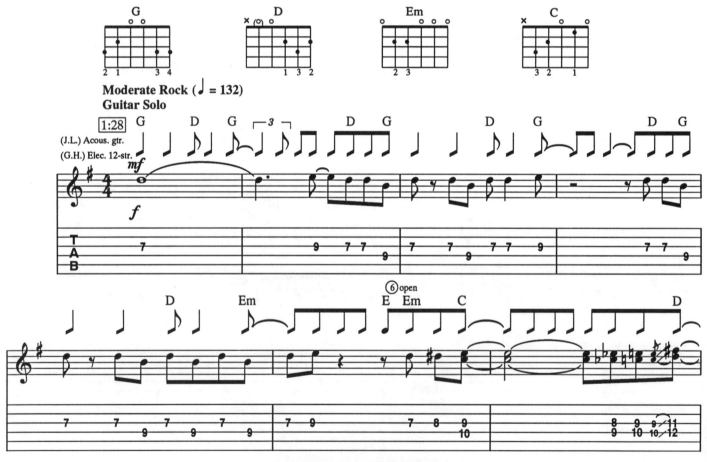

MCA music publishing

AND I LOVE HER

From the album _Hard Day's Night_
Words and Music by John Lennon and Paul McCartney

This is another Latin style number which utilizes both nylon and steel string acoustics and a 10-bar verse form. George's simple opening motif functions differently over the opening F#m to E6 chords, creating a nice tension/release effect. John's simple strumming pattern accompanies the first verse alone and is joined by George's arpeggiated figure on the second verse. This creates a lovely counterpoint part against the vocal melody. Again, note that the E6 chord in bar 13 is actually a C#m triad, which is the relative minor of E.

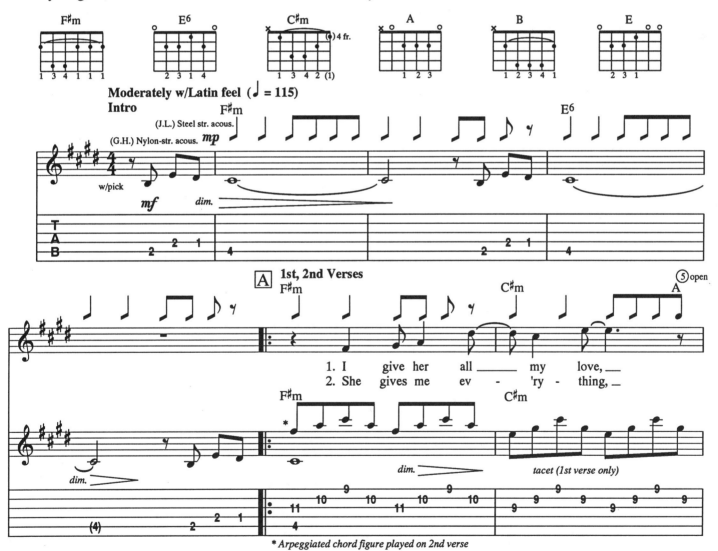

* Arpeggiated chord figure played on 2nd verse

AND I LOVE HER (Solo)

A dramatic 1/2 step modulation to the key of F sets the stage for George's poignant pick-style nylon-string acoustic solo, a rhythmically embellished restatement of the verse melody conceptually similar to the solo in "I Should Have Known Better." John's rhythm figure is peppered with open G6 passing chords to facilitate smooth fingering changes. The 3rd verse remains in the key of F, and subsequently features the counterpoint arpeggios heard in the 2nd verse transposed up 1/2 step.

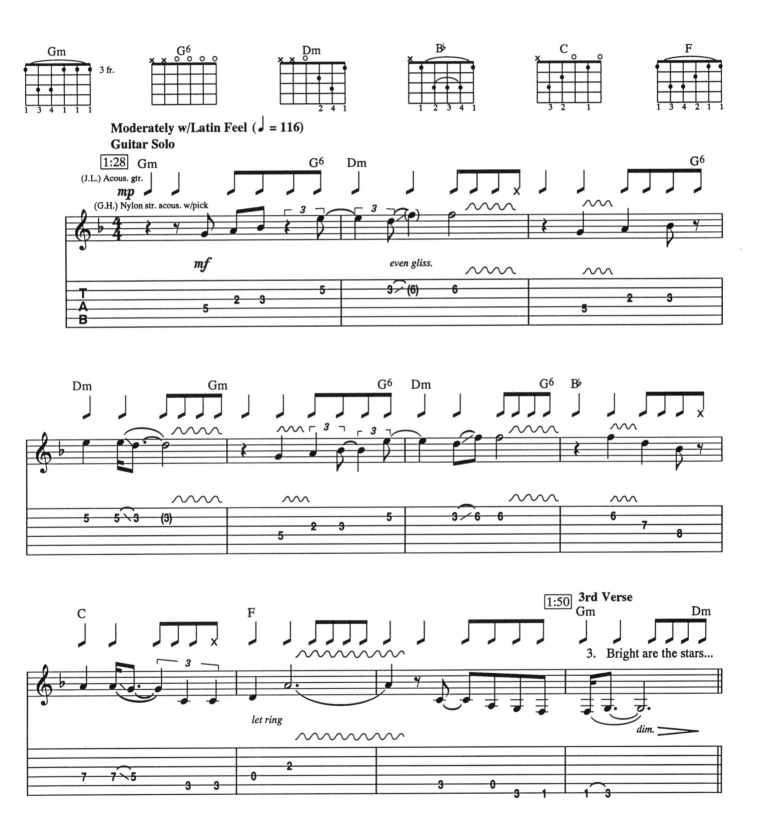

25

CAN'T BUY ME LOVE

From the album *Hard Day's Night*

Words and Music by John Lennon and Paul McCartney

Several call and response motifs are developed throughout George's bluesy 12-bar solo, which is played almost entirely in the 8th position using the C Pentatonic Minor scale. The IV chord is outlined in doublestops in bars 5 and 6; a descent into the 3rd position wraps up the solo. There are a number of bends throughout; not all of them hit their mark exactly, but these microtonal variations were part of George's sound. A strong swing feel undermines both the solo and John's alternating bass note/chord rhythm figure. When listening to the recording, you can occasionally hear remnants of a partially erased previous take.

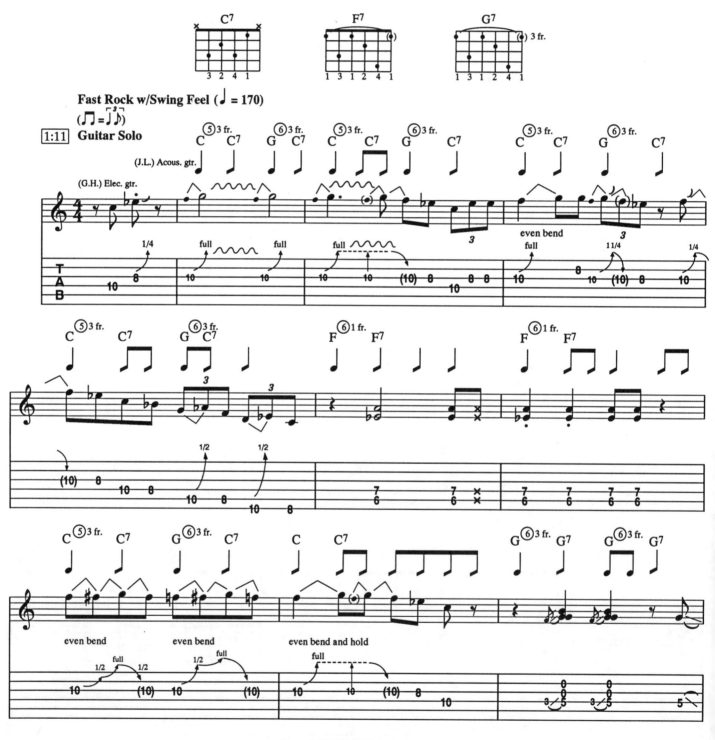

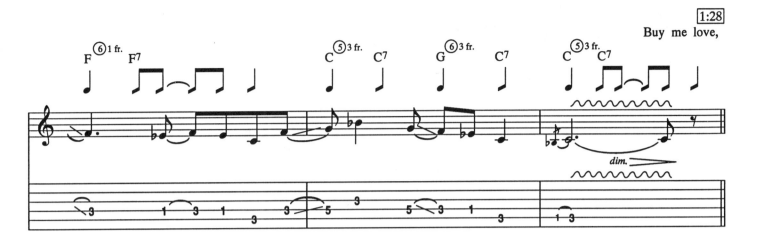

Buy me love,

YOU CAN'T DO THAT
From the album *Hard Day's Night*

Words and Music by John Lennon and Paul McCartney

In this signature intro figure, George's electric 12-string walks the thin line between major and minor tonalities by emphasizing both the ♭3rd (B♭) and ♮3rd (B♮). The entire 2-bar riff is played off of a 3rd position G chord voicing on the top four strings. John enters at the end of bar 2 with a whole step approach to the 3rd position G7 barre chord. He changes the voicing by simply lifting his pinky while maintaining the rest of the chord.

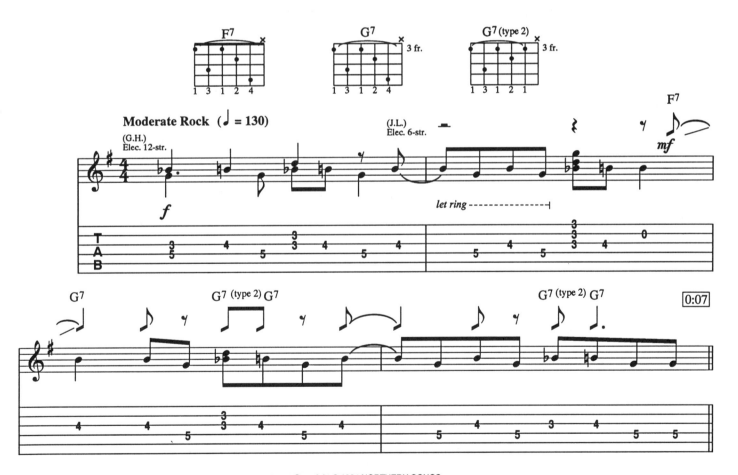

MCA music publishing

I FEEL FINE

From the album *Past Masters I*
Words and Music by John Lennon and Paul McCartney

Following a few seconds of open A-generated feedback, this intro riff is composed of a 2-bar phrase moved to three different positions outlining the V, IV and I chords in the key of G. The basic riff features an octave jump, a descension to the ♭7th and 5th and two suspension/resolutions utilizing the suspended 4th and 2nd. Again, the figure is based on a barre chord form which is held while notes are added with the pinky. Many doublestops occur randomly as the result of George's picking patterns but since the chord form is being maintained, any additional strings played will produce harmonious results. John doubles the riff in single notes.

I FEEL FINE (Solo)

George plays swing style eighth notes throughout his brief 4-bar solo. He kicks off with a motif that slides between two pairs of minor third intervals a whole step apart. The first pair functions as the 5th and ♭7th and moving this up two frets produces the 6th and root. The contrast between George's swing feel and John's straight-8th accompaniment creates a unique groove. George then lays out while John restates the main riff and waits until two bars before the start of the 3rd verse to re-enter.

SHE'S A WOMAN

From the album *Past Masters I*
Words and Music by John Lennon and Paul McCartney

A wide interval leap followed by a bluesy bent response characterizes the first 4 bars of George's solo. Bars 5-10 feature sliding 6ths played over the IV, I and V chords, concluding with a 5th position A pentatonic minor blues lick. John provides short chord chops on the backbeats ("2" and "4") throughout the 12-bar blues form.

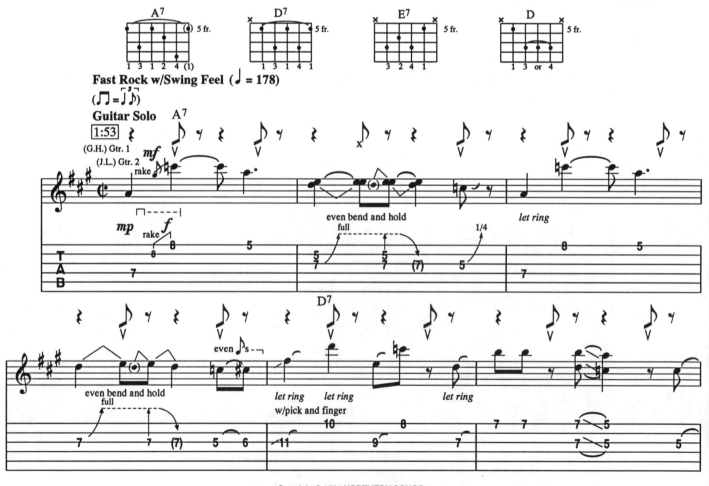

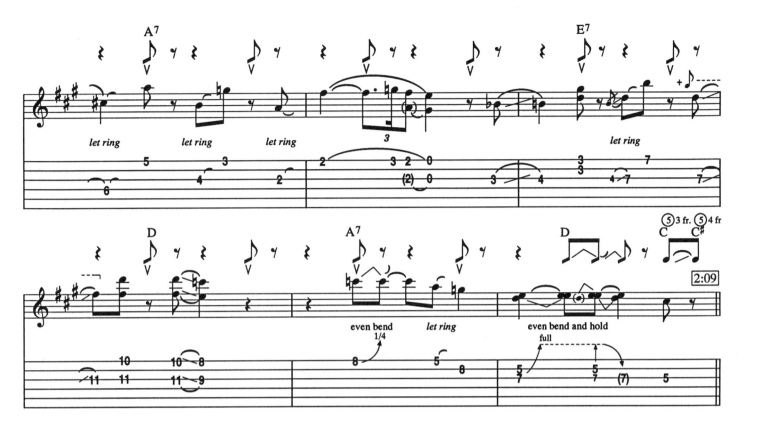

I'M A LOSER

From the album *Beatles For Sale*

Words and Music by John Lennon and Paul McCartney

After a scalewise climb into the 5th position, George used a hybrid pick/finger technique for this swinging, rockabilly/Chet Atkins-style 8-bar solo. Barre chord forms are used in the first 4 measures. The Bm7 voicing in bars 2 and 4 creates a D6 sound over John's D chord accompaniment. A wide interval skip implies a #9 over the G chord and is followed by an open Em7 lick. The solo concludes with a reverse Am arpeggio and a few doublestops where George gradually bends the ♭3rd up to the ♮3rd of a D chord. John's swing-8th rhythm figure propels the entire affair.

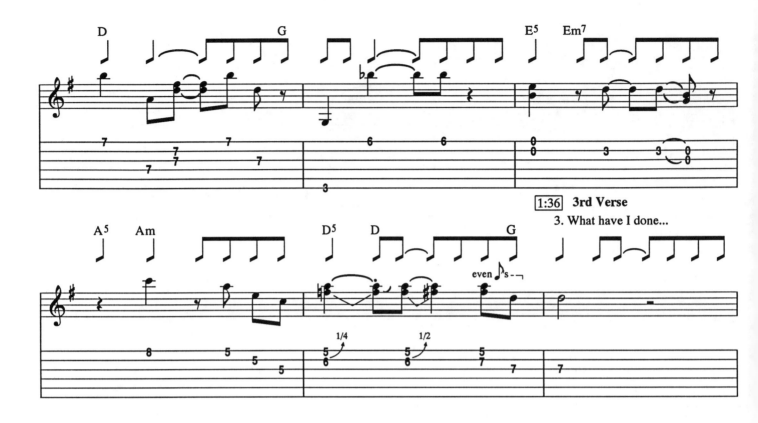

EIGHT DAYS A WEEK

From the album *Beatles For Sale*

Words and Music by John Lennon and Paul McCartney

This verse rhythm figure is a great example of how George and John worked off of each other rhythmically. John's acoustic part often features his alternating bass/chord technique in conjunction with a swing-8th note feel. George's electric chordings are played staccato-style for 8 bars before opening up for the following 4 bars. In this section, John accents "and 4" heavily with the drums. The final 4 bars of the progression return to the original feel. Note George's use of a chromatic passing chord between D and E.

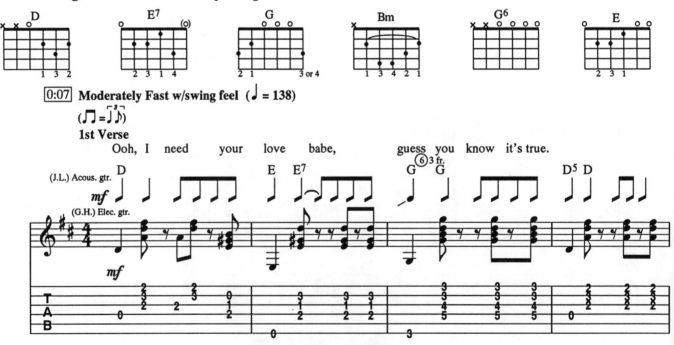

MCA music publishing

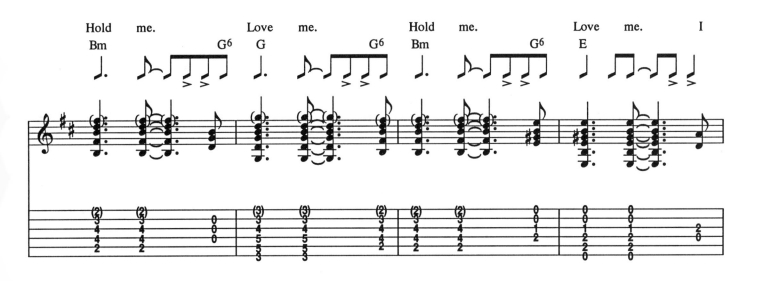

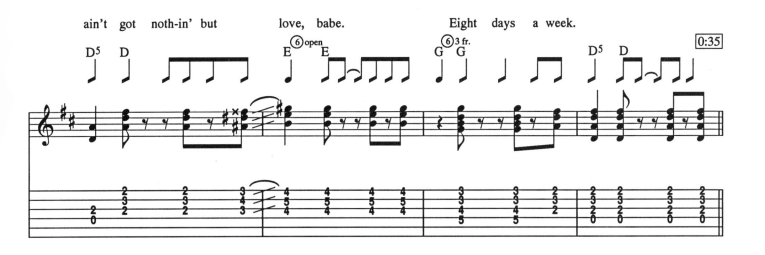

WORDS OF LOVE

From the album *Beatles For Sale*
Words and Music by Buddy Holly

The intro to this Buddy Holly tune slides from the 5th to the 2nd position using an open E pedal tone against fretted notes on the B string. An arpeggiated open D chord followed by an open E6 lick complete the 2-bar phrase, which is restated 4 times with a slight variation on the 4th repeat. The 1/2 step approach method is illustrated throughout John's rhythm part.

HONEY DON'T

From the album *Beatles For Sale*

Words and Music by Carl Lee Perkins

A descending line on the G string played against the open B and E strings forms the basis for George's intro to this Carl Perkins tune, which was the B-side of "Blue Suede Shoes." Don't forget to swing those eighth-notes.

YES IT IS

From the album *Past Masters I*
Words and Music by John Lennon and Paul McCartney

George introduced yet another technique on this lush, Motown-style ballad. Using a volume pedal to swell into open string harmonics creates a bell-like tone without a sharp attack. Harmonics also expand the guitar's upper range considerably. If you don't own a volume pedal, you can use your guitar's volume control instead. John's acoustic rhythm part is reminiscent of George's on "This Boy," without the staccato phrasing.

BAD BOY

From the album _Past Masters I_
Words and Music by Larry Williams

John and George's call and response intro paves the way for this Chuck Berry-style rocker. John's part is similar to the rhythm figures heard on "Hold Me Tight" and "I Call Your Name." George's responses are rooted in the 8th position C pentatonic minor scale.

I'M DOWN
From the album *Past Masters I*
Words and Music by John Lennon and Paul McCartney

This solo is played almost entirely in the 3rd position using the G pentatonic minor scale. A 2-bar motif is developed and moved over the IV chord before George adds a few frantic vibrato bar shakes to a repeated held bend, releases it and drops into the 1st position. The last bar of the solo features a slippery move between the 3rd and 1st positions.

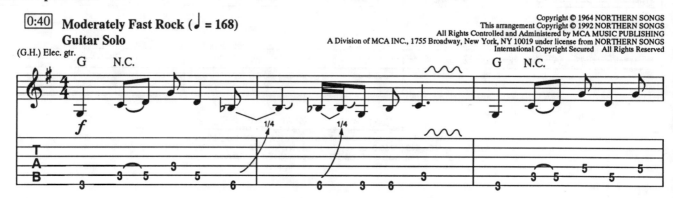

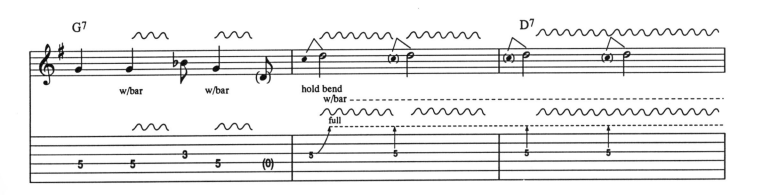

0:58 **3rd Verse**
3. We're all a-lone an' a - no-bod-y else.

HELP!

From the album *Help!*

Words and Music by John Lennon and Paul McCartney

This tune features a unique vocal intro not reprised anywhere else in the song. John's swing-eighth rhythm figure accompanies George's simple single-note descending bass line, setting up the straight-eighth signature arpeggio lick in bars 7 and 8. John's muted string slaps behind the lick are very effective.

MCA music publishing

THE NIGHT BEFORE

From the album *Help!*

Words and Music by John Lennon and Paul McCartney

What first appears to be a 12-string solo is revealed with close listening to be two double-tracked guitars playing in octaves. George mixes even and swing-style eighth notes throughout.

I NEED YOU

From the album *Help!*

Words and Music by George Harrison

Here's another example of George's volume pedal work. His part is based on the title phrase, playing first in unison with, then answering the lyric. John's pick-style nylon string acoustic accompaniment provides a tonal contrast to George's trebly electric sound. In the B section, he sustains 4-note chord voicings and articulates rhythmic accents with the volume pedal.

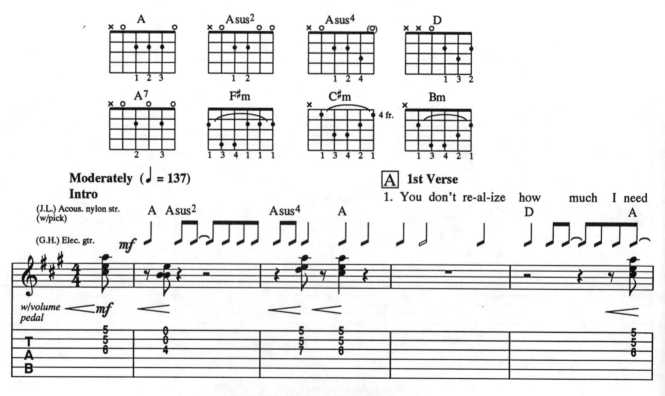

MCA music publishing

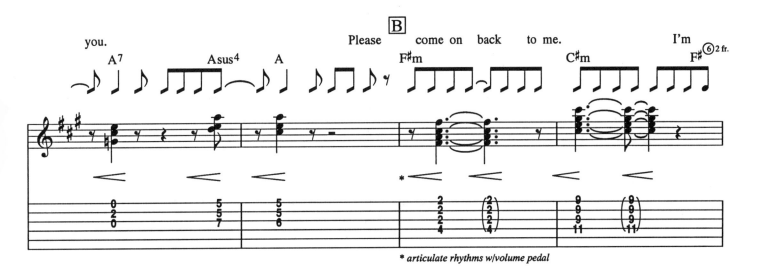

* articulate rhythms w/volume pedal

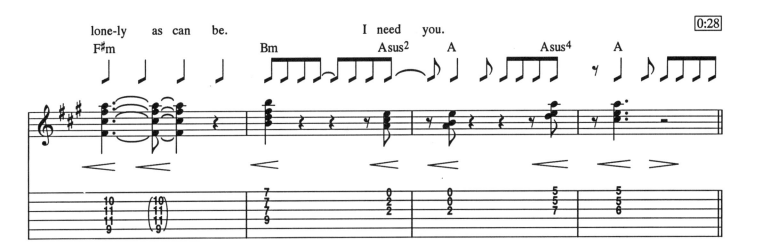

43

ACT NATURALLY

From the album *Help!*
Words and Music by Vonie Morrison and Johnny Russell

A descending scale line leads into George's hammer-on laden intro to Ringo's signature song. Bar 1 is fingered in the 5th position, bar 2 uses an embellished open D chord and bar 3 is played around a 3rd position G chord voicing before concluding with a 3rd finger slide lick. This country-swing flavor is further enhanced by John's rhythm playing, also peppered with hammered fills within chord forms.

DIZZY MISS LIZZIE

From the album *Help!*

Words and Music by Larry Williams

George gets a lot of mileage out of a simple 10th position riff in this rocker; he also rarely plays it exactly the same way twice. John's solid rhythm part recalls "Hold Me Tight" and "Bad Boy," and the key of A offers the opportunity to play the figure through the I, IV and V chords without leaving open position.

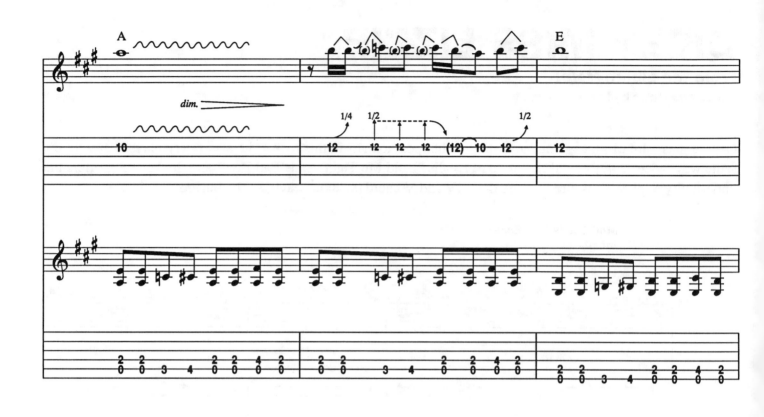

0:22

1. You make me diz-zy, Miss...

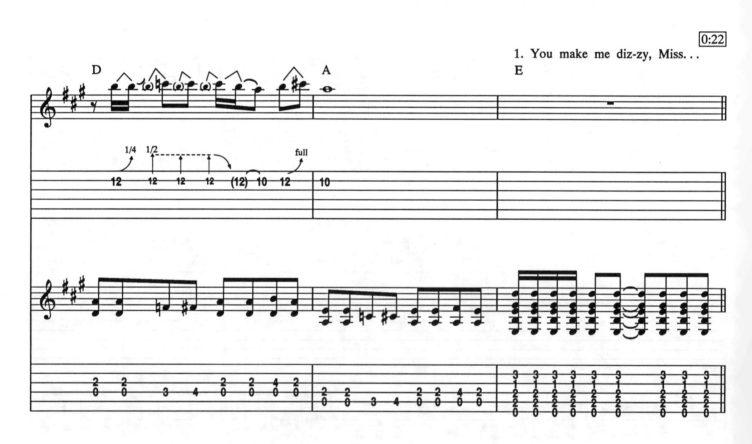

DAY TRIPPER

From the album *Past Masters II*
Words and Music by John Lennon and Paul McCartney

Both guitars begin this signature 2-bar riff in unison. The bass enters on the first repeat and John breaks off into a chordal rhythm figure at bar 5. A tambourine playing 16th-notes with accents on beats "2" and "4" adds rhythmic propulsion until the drums enter. The tambourine pulls back to a steady eighth-note rhythm featuring similar accents.

WE CAN WORK IT OUT

From the album *Past Masters II*

Words and Music by John Lennon and Paul McCartney

John's acoustic rhythm part is based on a 16th-note strum pattern. Playing all the eighth-notes as downstrokes will naturally place all 16th-note upbeats on upstrokes. When strumming quarter and eighth notes or the hammered 16th note sus4 figures go through the motions of playing every 16th note while only attacking the strings on the appropriate beats.

DRIVE MY CAR

From the album *Rubber Soul*

Words and Music by John Lennon and Paul McCartney

A curious metric figure kicks off this R & B style rave-up. Though George seems to begin his intro lick on beat 4, Paul's subsequent bass fill seems to land squarely on beat 1 of the 2nd measure. This leaves nine eighth notes before the downbeat of the verse figure, creating a measure of 9/8. Whether this was intentional is questionable, but it makes the most sense from a notational standpoint. The verse rhythm figure features an Otis Redding-inspired single-note low register riff built on an alternating I to IV (D to G) root movement. Bars 9 and 10 (actually the 7th and 8th of the verse) use a V chord build-up to create momentum into the chorus. The chorus is in B minor which contains the same notes as the relative major key of D. With the piano providing chordal accompaniment, the guitar part sticks to doubling the bass line throughout.

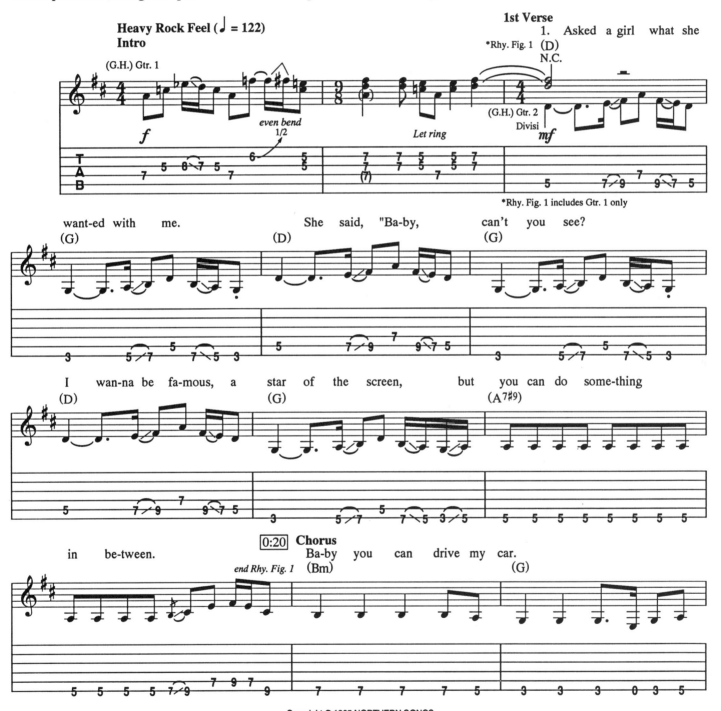

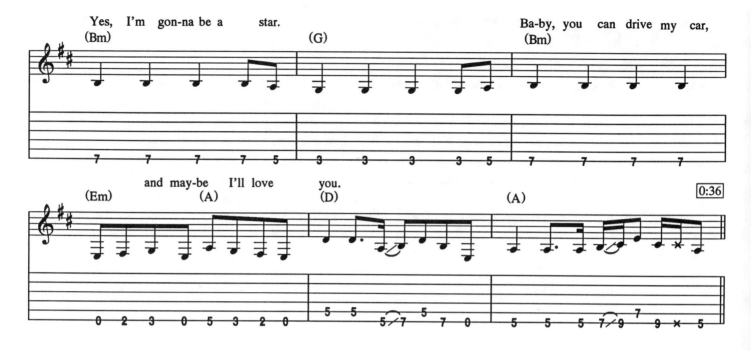

DRIVE MY CAR (Solo)

It sounds as though Paul McCartney played the high D notes (not always exactly on target) with a slide worn on his pinky, leaving his remaining fingers free to fret and bend notes conventionally. It's possible that they were string bends but the giveaway here seems to lie in the last two bars, which are definitely slide. As we will soon see, Paul was responsible for several of the Beatles' wildest guitar solos.

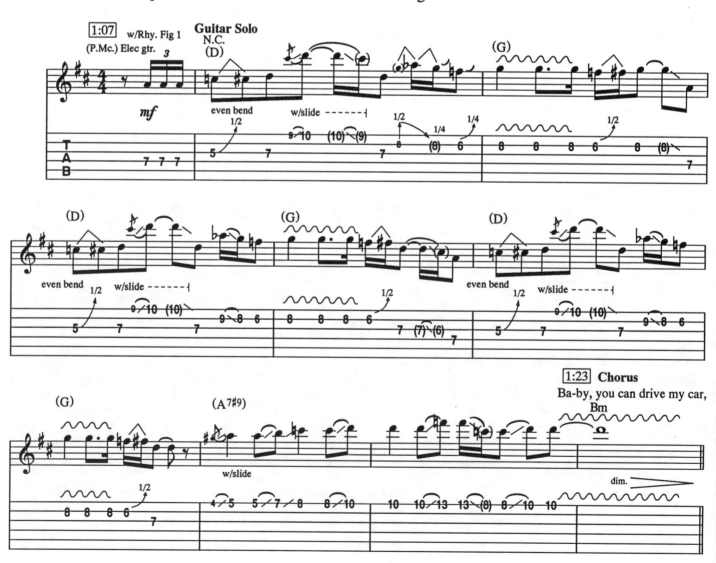

YOU WON'T SEE ME

From the album *Rubber Soul*

Words and Music by John Lennon and Paul McCartney

This verse excerpt illustrates how effective simple Stax-style backbeat "chops" can be behind a strong melody. Ringo's extremely cool beat ties it all together.

MCA music publishing

NOWHERE MAN

From the album *Rubber Soul*

Words and Music by John Lennon and Paul McCartney

George's lovely chord melody style solo seems to shimmer due to an unusual amount of added compression and boosted top end on his Sonic blue Fender Stratocaster. Each phrase is built around a chord form until the final 2 bars, where a single note bass figure leads to the tonic low E. This is answered by an E natural harmonic 4 octaves higher. John's part is played with a capo at the 2nd fret. The A6 chord preceding many chord changes is the transposed equivalent of the open G6 "all-purpose" passing chord.

MCA music publishing

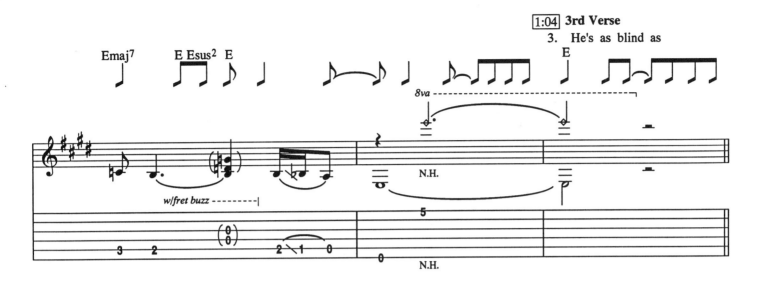

THE WORD
From the album *Rubber Soul*
Words and Music by John Lennon and Paul McCartney

George's 2-note voicings create a rich dominant 7#9 sound against the piano figure throughout this opening chorus excerpt. Placing the second accent on the "and" of beat 3 creates a variation of the basic Stax-style backbeat part found in "You Won't See Me." In bars 12 and 13, (actually bars 9 and 10 of the verse) the guitar accents are in unison with the vocal line before returning to 2 bars of staccato chops, completing the 12-bar form. The funky unison line doubled throughout the 4-bar verse also has a Stax/Motown flavor.

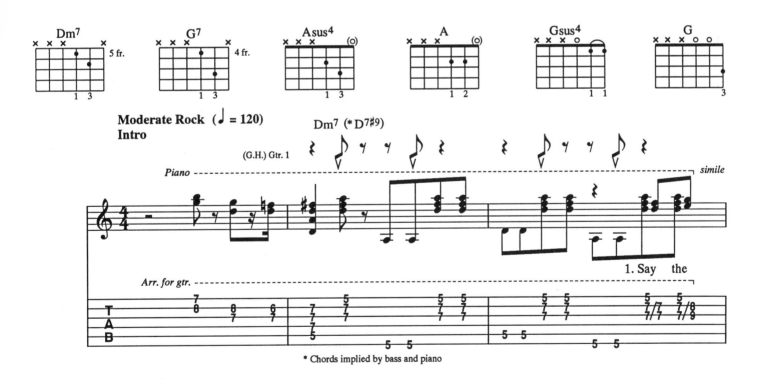

* Chords implied by bass and piano

MCA music publishing

but now I've got it, the word is good. — Spread the (word)

MICHELLE

From the album *Rubber Soul*
Words and Music by John Lennon and Paul McCartney

This dual acoustic intro in Fm segues to an F major verse progression.

GIRL

From the album *Rubber Soul*

Words and Music by John Lennon and Paul McCartney

This tune is played at a moderate tempo with a swing feel. Capoing at the 8th fret gives John's rhythm part a tight, almost Nashville-tuned quality. The "open" (8th fret) E♭6 chords found throughout are the transposed equivalent of the G6 all-purpose passing chord in the open position. His overdubbed acoustic guitar provides a nice counterpoint part to the vocal melody. The line features an ascending sequence of 3rd intervals diatonic to the key of C minor (relative to E♭ major) followed by a sequenced scale-wise return to its starting point. Note that this part is played entirely on the 2nd and 3rd strings.

GIRL (Interlude)

A shift to a straight 8th/16th feel sets the stage for this 8-bar interlude featuring all of the previous parts embellished by George's acoustic 12-string figure. Playing even 8th notes, he adds a 3rd harmony part above John's original counterpoint line. A psuedo-bazouki effect is created by playing this part on the unison-tuned top two strings. The following brief return to the chorus resumes a swing feel through the fadeout.

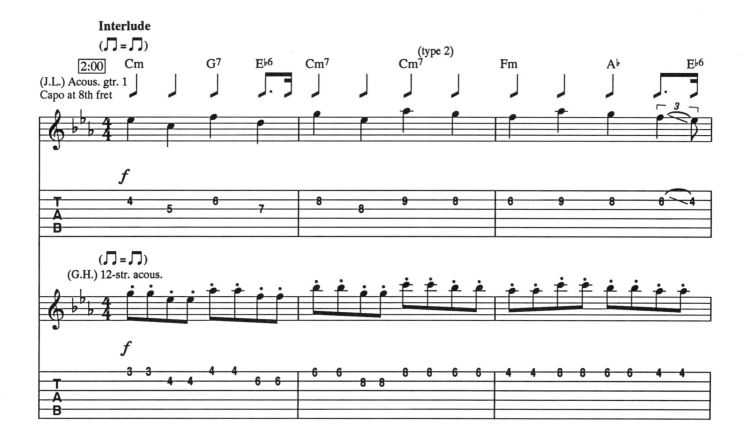

57

WAIT

From the album *Rubber Soul*

Words and Music by John Lennon and Paul McCartney

George's volume pedal swells were obviously culled from the vocal part of each 3-bar verse phrase.

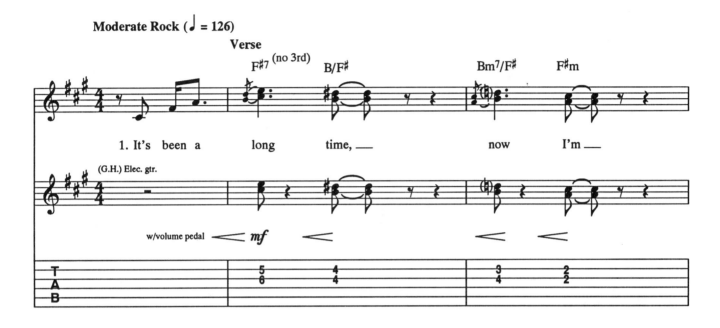

PAPERBACK WRITER

From the album *Rubber Soul*
Words and Music by John Lennon and Paul McCartney

John called this tune "Son of 'Day Tripper," meaning a rock 'n' roll song with a guitar lick on a fuzzy, loud guitar. George's signature intro lick is played in the 3rd position.

TAXMAN

From the album *Revolver*
Words and Music by George Harrison

George's rhythm part is developed and embellished with each subsequent verse throughout "Taxman." Built on a 13-bar form, the 1st verse features 3-note D7 voicings (sometimes preceded by a single D note) on beats "2" and "4" with two accented $D7\sharp9$ chords on the 3rd bar of the first two 4-bar phrases. The move to C and G chords suggest D Mixolydian (relative to G major) more than D major. This part has been labeled "Rhy. Fig. 1."

On the second verse, the D note preceding the chordal accent on beat 4 becomes a staple part, creating a slight variation from the 1st verse. Following the guitar solo, an overdubbed single-note riff is introduced and played in conjunction with Rhy. Fig. 1. The 1-bar lick repeats, then rests for 2 bars while the "Ah, ah, Mister Wilson," vocals respond. This 4-bar phrase is repeated before the lick is transposed down a whole step over 2 bars of C, then down a perfect 4th (2 1/2 steps) over G. The 2-bar return to the tonic D features a variation which sets up the new part for the 4th verse. Here, only the first 12 bars of Rhy. Fig. 1 are played since two bars have been added to the progression. The slash rhythms above the staff notate the changes leading to Paul's outro solo.

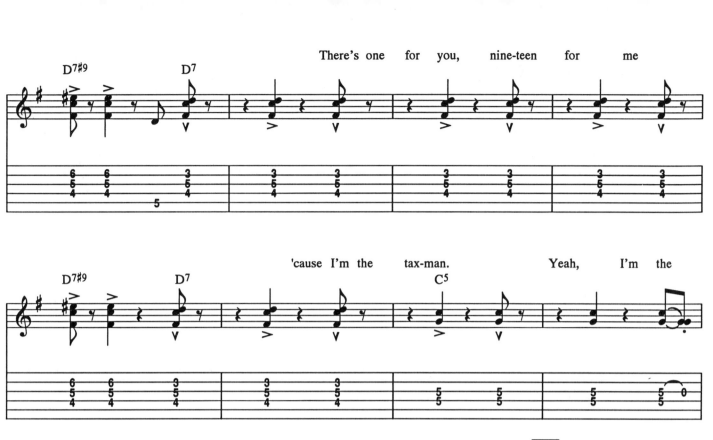

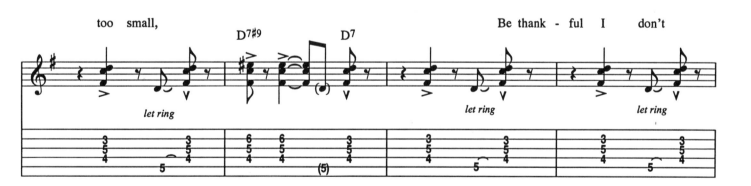

TAXMAN (Solo)

Paul McCartney's wild Hendrix-influenced solo is played almost entirely on the 2nd and 3rd strings. Paul seems to prefer playing along a single string's length to playing across strings in a fixed pattern. His crammed rhythmic phrases, use of open strings and note choices create a modal, almost raga-like effect. The unusual positions reflect the bassist's unique conception of the guitar fingerboard. The outro solo heard after the 4th verse was actually this same performance "flown in" to the track for the fadeout.

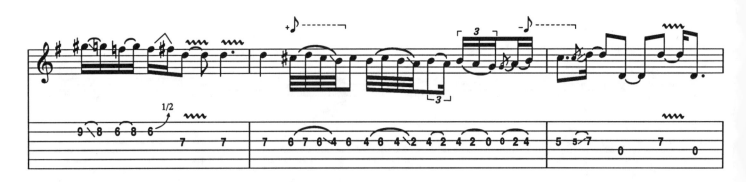

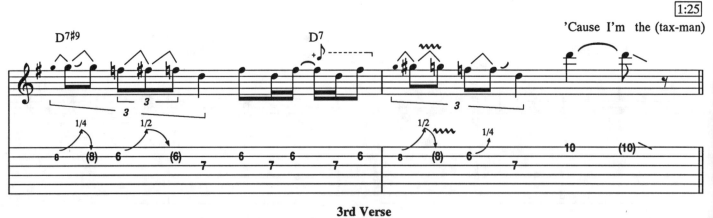

(Ah, ah, Mis-ter Wil-son)   if you don't want to   pay   some   more,

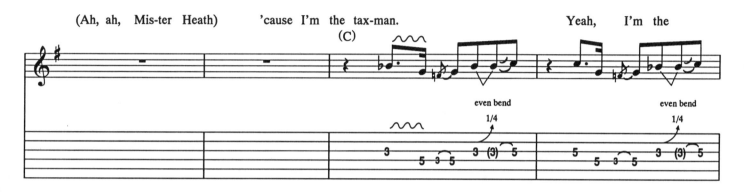

(Ah, ah, Mis-ter Heath)   'cause I'm the tax-man.   Yeah,   I'm the

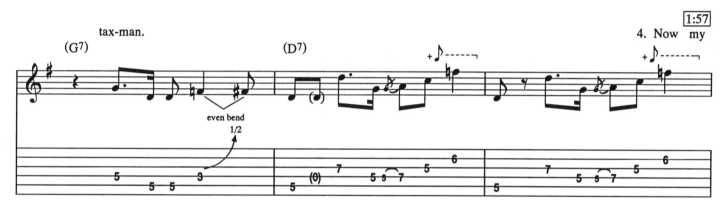

tax-man.   4. Now my

4th Verse

1:58   w/Rhy. Fig. 1 (1st 12 bars only)

ad-vice   for   those   who   die,   (Tax-man.)   de-clare

the   pen-nies   on   your   eyes,   (Tax-man.)   'cause I'm the

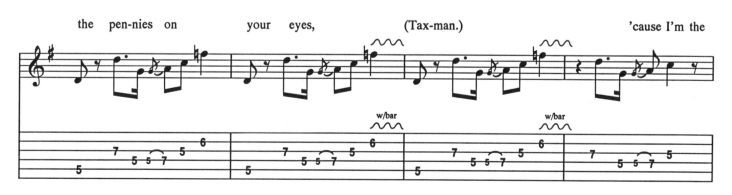

I'M ONLY SLEEPING

From the album *Revolver*

Words and Music by John Lennon and Paul McCartney

A moderate loping swing feel pervades this dreamy verse excerpt featuring John's heavily compressed 12-string acoustic. The 15-bar verse feels very natural as the ingenious chord progression floats between minor and major tonalities. George's reverse tape fills later in the song were among the first recorded examples of that effect.

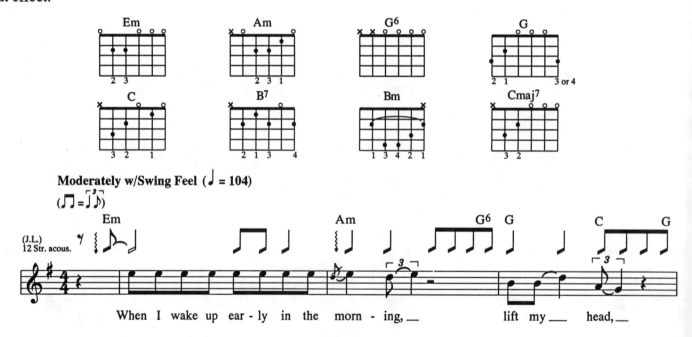

I'm still yawn - ing. When I'm in the mid - dle of a dream,

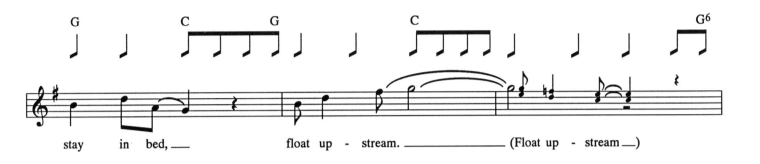

stay in bed, ___ float up - stream. _____ (Float up - stream ___)

Please don't wake ___ me. No, ___ don't shake ___ me, Leave ___ me where ___ I am, ___

___ I'm on - ly sleep - ing. ___

HERE, THERE AND EVERYWHERE

From the album *Revolver*

Words and Music by John Lennon and Paul McCartney

Paul's verse accompaniment consists of partially arpeggiated chord shapes. The G, Am, Bm, C, Em and D7 chords are diatonic to the key of G, while F$\sharp$m^7 and B^7 are borrowed from the relative key of E minor.

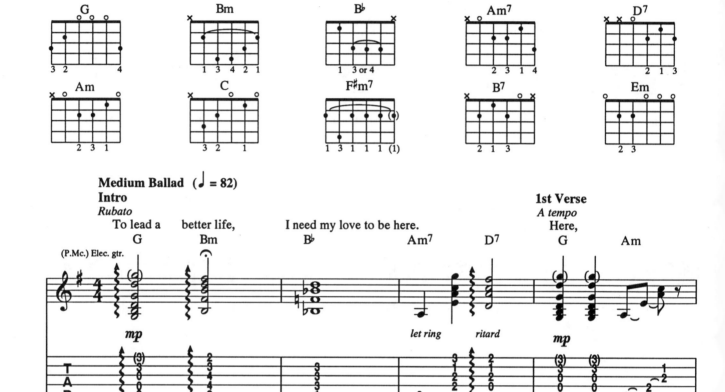

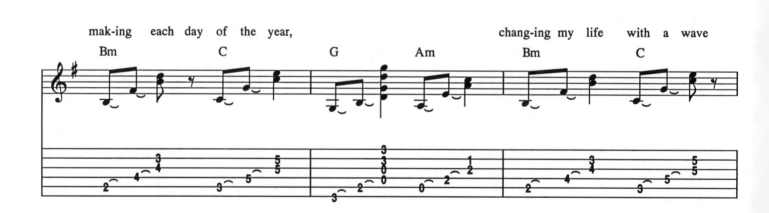

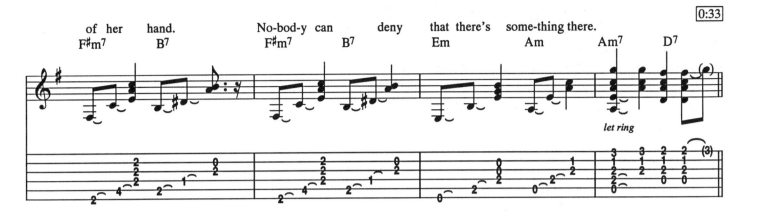

of her hand.   No-bod-y can   deny   that there's   some-thing there.

SHE SAID SHE SAID

From the album *Revolver*
Words and Music by John Lennon and Paul McCartney

George's signature fuzztone riff is actually a rhythmically displaced quote of the third phrase of the vocal melody ("I Know What It Is To Be Sad.") The vocal part begins on beat "3" while the intro riff starts on "1." John moves a voice within a capoed B♭ voicing to create B♭7 and picks some nice 16th note syncopations.

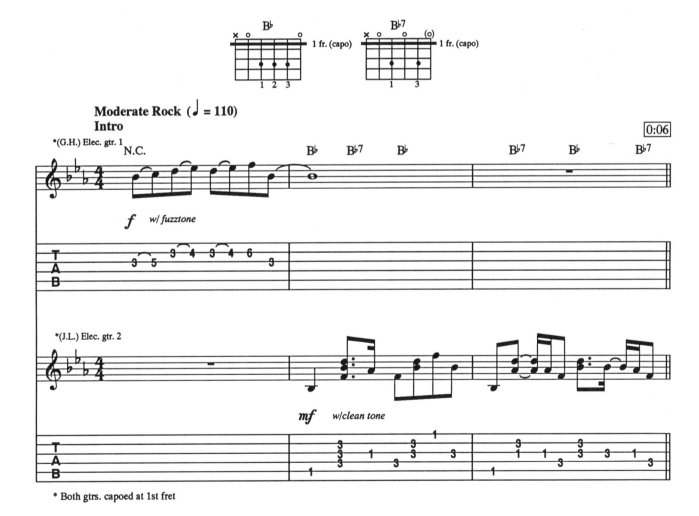

Moderate Rock (♩ = 110)
Intro

* Both gtrs. capoed at 1st fret

AND YOUR BIRD CAN SING

From the album *Revolver*

Words and Music by John Lennon and Paul McCartney

It's difficult to pin down who played what on this one. George has recalled in print that he remembers playing "quite a complicated little line that goes right through the middle eight" with John or Paul! This entire excerpt is heard twice in the song. The first 4 bars also serve as the intro. Derived entirely from the key of E, the opening 2 bars begin with diatonic 3rd harmonies before moving to gradually widening harmonies reminiscent of an English horn fox call. This occurs on beat "3" of the 2nd measure, where the harmonies move from a 3rd to a 4th, then a 6th to a 5th. The harmonies are mixed over the next 2 bars and move on to the final 4 bars, which feature diatonic 6th harmonies.

MCA music publishing

I WANT TO TELL YOU

From the album *Revolver*

Words and Music by George Harrison

This signature riff fade-in uses open A and D pedal tones against a series of descending pull-offs on the 3rd and 4th strings. Note that the 2-bar phrase actually begins at the double bar line and that the eighth notes are played with a swing feel.

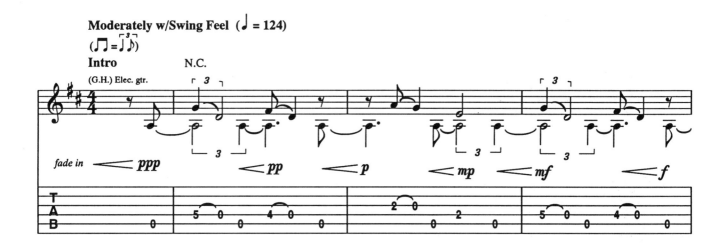

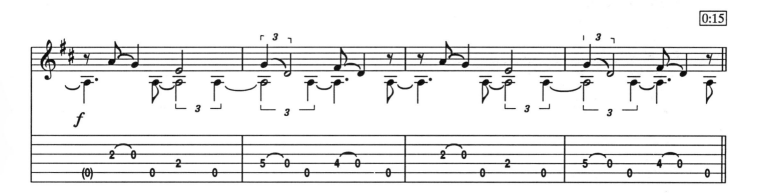

WITH A LITTLE HELP FROM MY FRIENDS

From the album *Sgt. Pepper's Lonely Hearts Club Band*

Words and Music by John Lennon and Paul McCartney

The elaborate production on the "Sgt. Pepper's. . ." album marked the start of a more orchestrated approach to guitar parts that was to become integrated throughout the rest of the Beatles' career. George's intro features two whole-step approaches to the tonic E chord, (C to D) each voiced with the 5th in the bass. Over the E chord, he picks a series of descending 3rds on the 2nd and 3rd strings while allowing the open 1st string to ring. The verse and chorus progressions are outlined by simple staccato quarter note accents through the majestic overdubbed fill at bar 18. Remember to swing those 8ths.

MCA music publishing

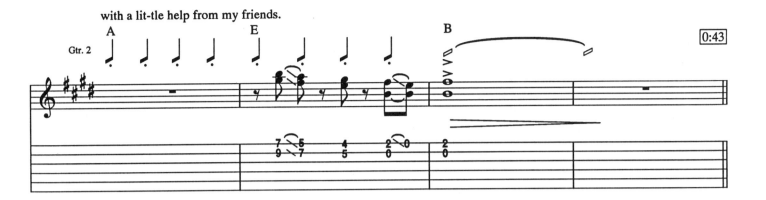

LUCY IN THE SKY WITH DIAMONDS

From the album *Sgt. Pepper's Lonely Hearts Club Band*
Words and Music by John Lennon and Paul McCartney

John's signature 6/8 keyboard part has been arranged here for guitar and is primarily played in the 9th position. His electric part in the B section features repeated attacks on a held bend which mimic the vocal melody. The rhythmic transition and key modulation to the 4/4 C section are masterstrokes. Here, the quarter note takes on the value of two eighth notes from the 6/8 B section. John's electric chorus figure utilizes a major scale ascension to a 16th note based V chord (D) figure. A studio-flanged acoustic guitar is also present throughout the B and C sections.

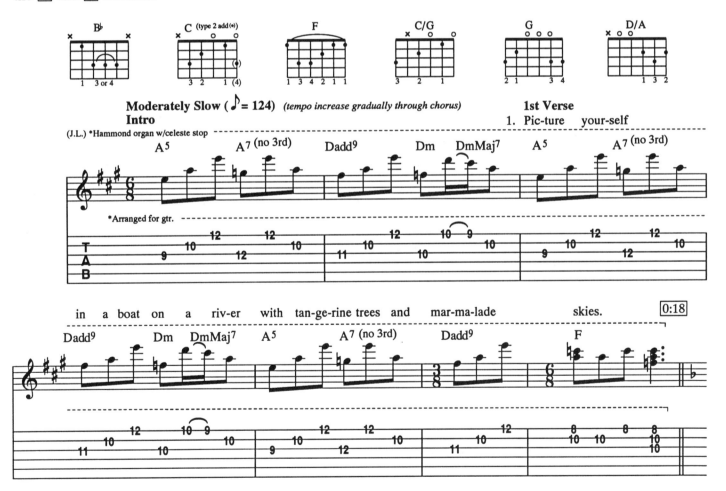

MCA music publishing

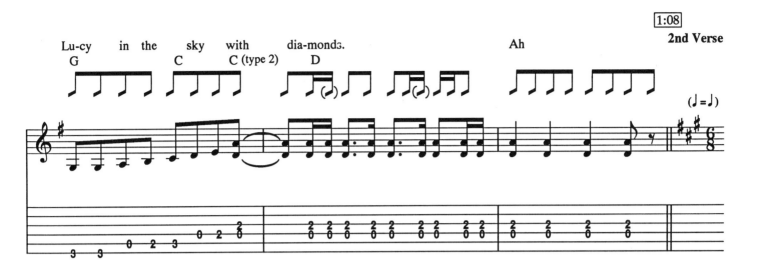

Lu-cy in the sky with dia-monds.   Ah

G   C   C (type 2)   D

GETTING BETTER

From the album *Sgt. Pepper's Lonely Hearts Club Band*
Words and Music by John Lennon and Paul McCartney

John's high octave G's create an added 9th over George's F chord in this intro, giving it a suspended sound. As George changes to the tonic C for the verse, the octaves switch roles and function as the 5th. Another suspension is followed by the V chord where the octaves now serve as the tonic. An instrumental response to the vocal is established in bar 6 as the octaves are impossibly sustained. The figure developed over bars 9-12 sounds like a slo-mo Chuck Berry chordal riff. The high octave G's return for the chorus and function as the following intervals over the electric piano harmony (which has been arranged here for guitar): 5th of C, 4th of Dm, ♭3rd of Em and 9th of F.

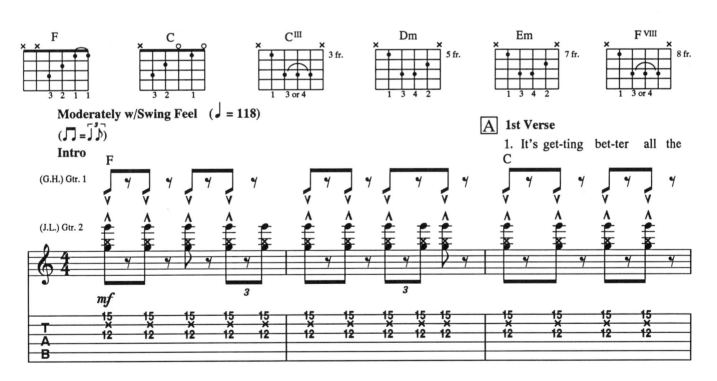

MCA music publishing

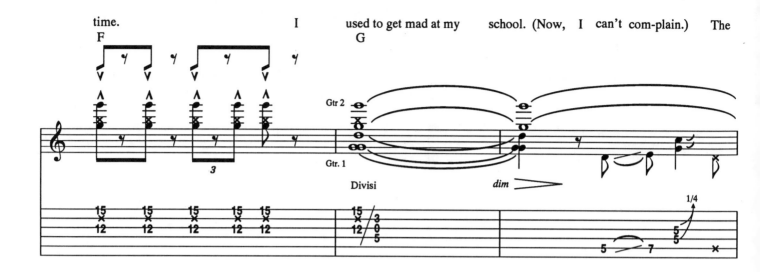

time. I used to get mad at my school. (Now, I can't com-plain.) The

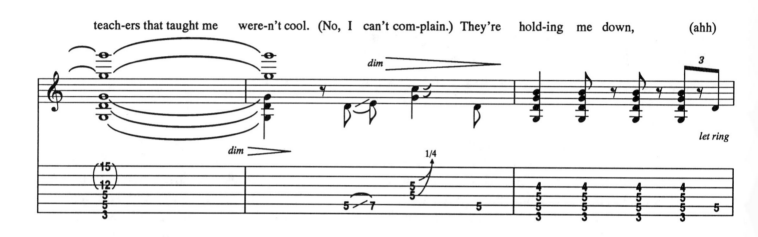

teach-ers that taught me were-n't cool. (No, I can't com-plain.) They're hold-ing me down, (ahh)

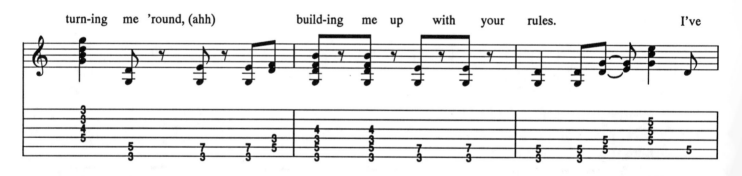

turn-ing me 'round, (ahh) build-ing me up with your rules. I've

B Chorus

got to ad-mit, it's get-ting bet-ter, a lit-tle bet-ter all the time.

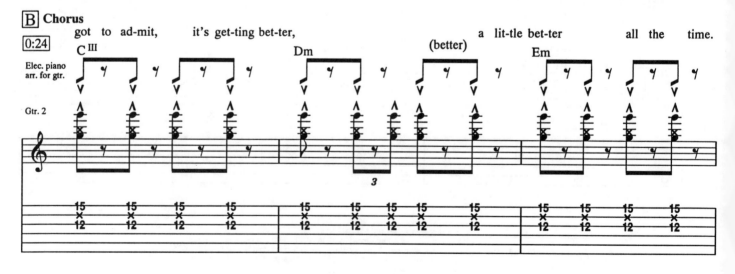

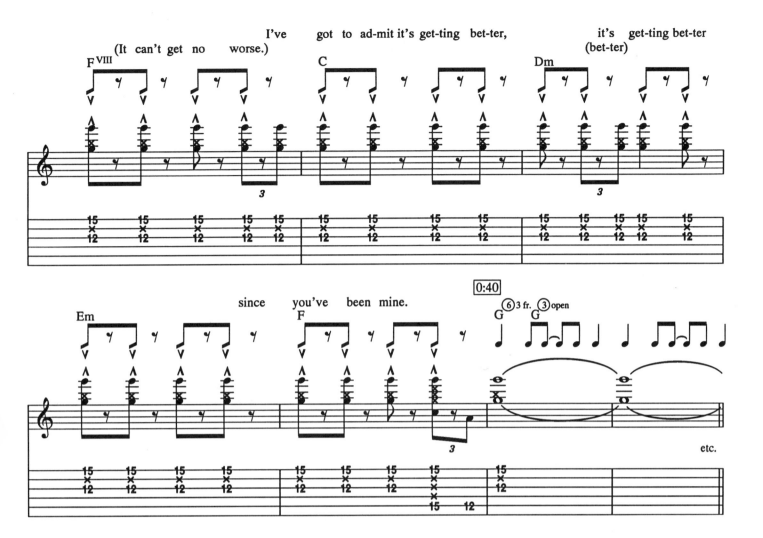

FIXING A HOLE

From the album *Sgt. Pepper's Lonely Hearts Club Band*

Words and Music by John Lennon and Paul McCartney

Dropping the 6th string to D will allow you to cover the orchestrated fills, the Ⓒ section rhythm figure and the solo to this McCartney tune. George's double-tracked fills outline an F minor chord and are arranged in a way that makes them playable on one guitar. The Ⓒ section figure doubles the bass line before adding a nicely phrased ascending scale line. His solo is also double-tracked and creates the illusion of unison open and fretted strings played simultaneously, especially in the first two bars. Note the many eighth note syncopations throughout. The concluding bass-register riff also makes use of the dropped D tuning to create a larger-than-life effect.

1. I'm fix - ing a hole __ where the rain __ gets __ in __ and stops my mind __ from wan -
fill - ing the cracks that __ ran __ through the door and kept my mind __ from wan -

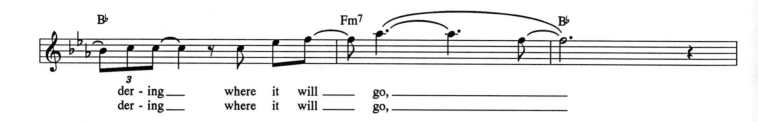

der - ing____ where it will ____ go, _____
der - ing____ where it will ____ go, _____

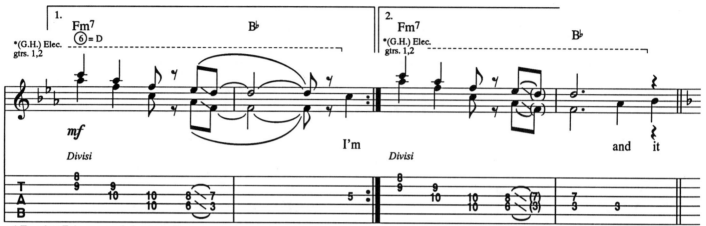

1.
*(G.H.) Elec.
gtrs. 1,2
mf
Divisi
I'm

2.
*(G.H.) Elec.
gtrs. 1,2
Divisi
and it

* Tune low E down one whole step to D

B Gtrs. tacet

real - ly does - n't mat - ter if I'm wrong____ I'm right where I be - long____

____ I'm right where I be-long, ____

See the peo - ple stand - ing there who dis - a - gree _(and) nev - er win and

Gtr. 1

won-der why they don't get in my ____ door. ____ 2. I'm paint-ing a room____ in a col-

FIXING A HOLE (Solo)

1:16 Moderate Swing (♩ = 115)

Guitar Solo

1:33

And it

GOOD MORNING GOOD MORNING

From the album *Sgt. Pepper's Lonely Hearts Club Band*

Words and Music by John Lennon and Paul McCartney

These common chord forms are put through some odd paces as almost every measure changes time signatures in this verse excerpt. Listening to the horn section in the following verses will help you lock in on this part. The G/A open string passing chord serves the same function as the often-used G6. The interaction between this figure and the vocal melody is definitely worth scrutinizing.

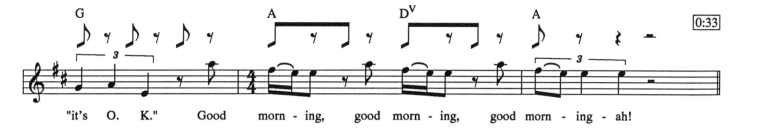

"it's O. K." Good morn - ing, good morn - ing, good morn - ing - ah!

GOOD MORNING GOOD MORNING (Solo)

Paul unleashes another fuzztone raga-like solo excursion played almost entirely on the B string. As in "Taxman," he moves along the string length tossing in an occasional open string very much in the Hendrix tradition. Paul fills around the vocal line before wrapping up with a wide interval skip and even bend from G to A.

1:16 Moderately (♩ = 122)

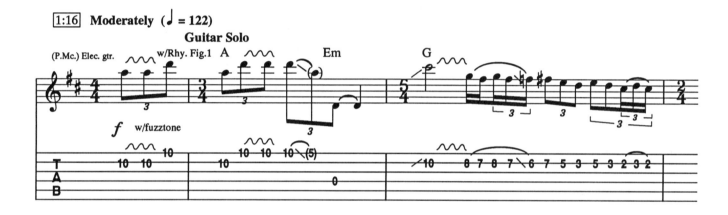

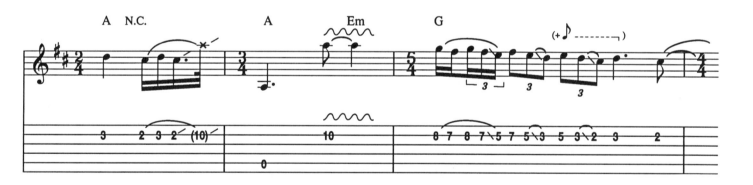

Peo-ple run-nin' 'round, it's five o'clock. Eve-ry-where in town is get-ting dark.

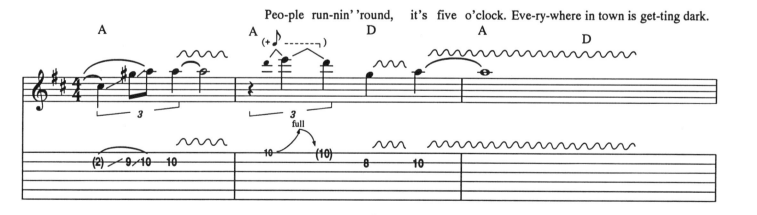

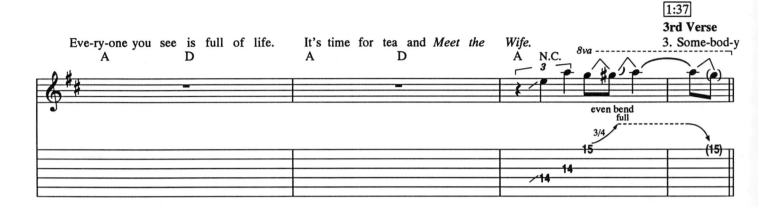

HELLO, GOODBYE

From the album *Magical Mystery Tour*

Words and Music by John Lennon and Paul McCartney

The guitar parts in the **Magical Mystery Tour** album were even more precisely arranged than on **"Sgt. Pepper's..."** In fact, guitars were entirely absent from many songs. In this verse and chorus excerpt, the guitar plays a simple reverse bend in response to the vocal melody and rests until the chorus. The counterpoint chorus line is played twice with a slight variation on the repeat. Note that the verse figure is 8 1/2 bars long, (counting the 2/4 bar) while the chorus spans 7 measures.

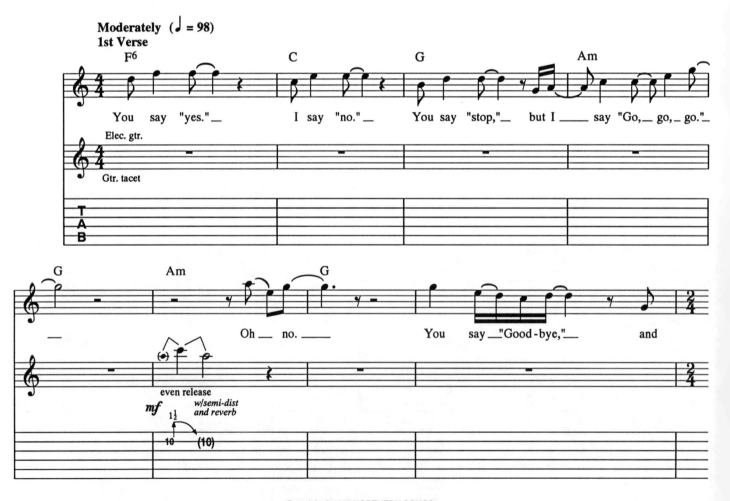

MCA music publishing

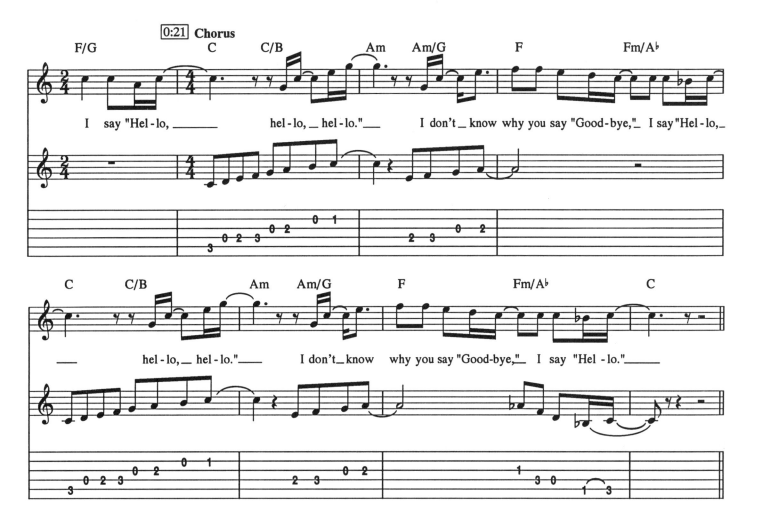

THE FOOL ON THE HILL

From the album *Magical Mystery Tour*
Words and Music by John Lennon and Paul McCartney

In this excerpt, George's acoustic guitar plays a short but sweet counterpoint line against the vocal melody. The up and downstemmed parts may have been recorded separately.

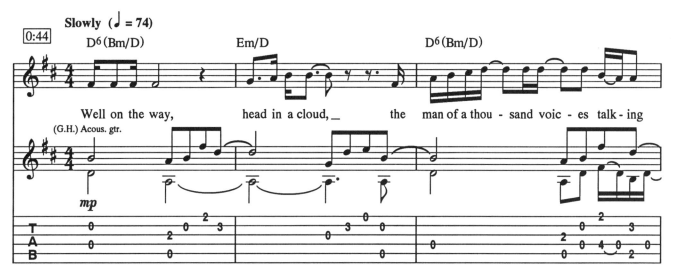

MCA music publishing

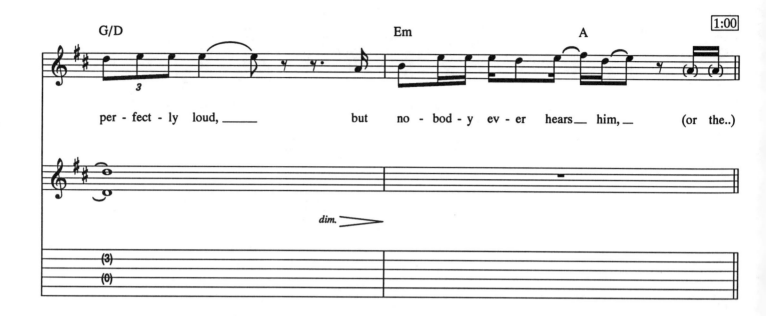

per - fect - ly loud, _____ but no - bod - y ev - er hears __ him, __ (or the..)

FLYING

From the album *Magical Mystery Tour*
Words and Music by John Lennon, Paul McCartney, George Harrison and Richard Starkey

Reportedly the first tune written equally by all four Beatles, this dreamy 12-bar progression was given an eerie touch with the use of a Mellotron's pitch control. In the guitar department, George uses a heavily tremolo-laden sound and seemingly rakes almost every chord he plays. The I chord figure features alternating $Csus^4$ and C chords while the IV and V chords are played straight. John's compressed but dry acoustic lead enters at bar 6 playing doublestops in 3rds before resting for a bar. He concludes this 12-bar chorus with a string of sliding 6ths built off the V and IV chords.

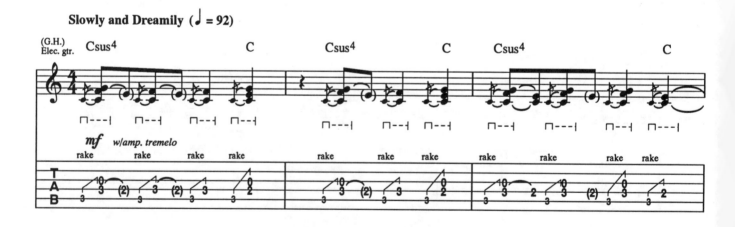

LADY MADONNA

From the album *Magical Mystery Tour*
Words and Music by John Lennon and Paul McCartney

This walking bass figure in open position outlines the I and IV chords against Paul's ace boogie-woogie piano playing. Notice how the ascending scale line leading back to the tonic uses F♮. The excerpt at ⌐1:15⌐ is George's very cool 1 1/2 beat pickup back into the main riff.

MCA music publishing

REVOLUTION

Single version from *Past Masters II*
Words and Music by John Lennon and Paul McCartney

One of the three recorded "Revolutions," this single version had the most fuzzed-out intro of all. John plugged in direct, persuaded the engineer to overload the console inputs on this guitar and voice to the max and ripped into this Chuck Berry-on-acid style intro. The verse rhythm figure is established at bar 5 and quickly settles into the 2nd position using an ingenious hammer-on pattern.

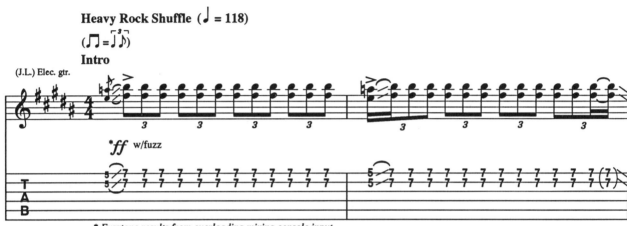

* *Fuzztone results from overloading mixing console input.*

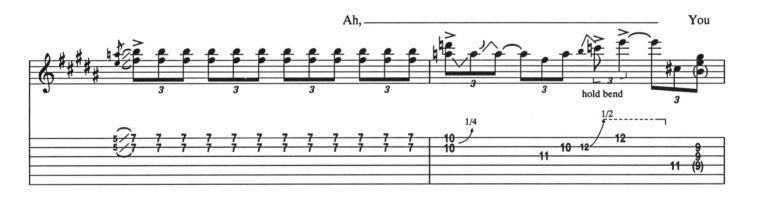

HEY BULLDOG

From the album *Yellow Submarine*
Words and Music by John Lennon and Paul McCartney

John's piano pounds out this memorable 2-bar signature riff and is subsequently joined by himself and George doubling on guitars. Paul enters at bar 5, creating a powerful and memorable intro. The tune was covered by Fanny in the mid-70's.

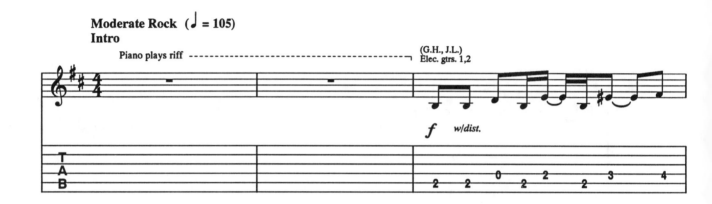

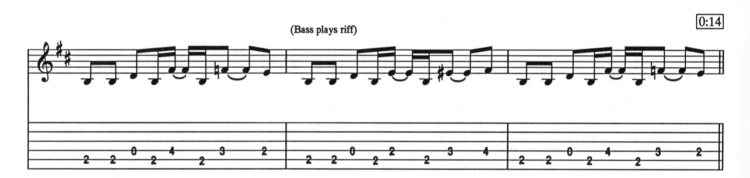

DEAR PRUDENCE

From the album *The Beatles*

Words and Music by John Lennon and Paul McCartney

John and George overdubbed the guitars on this song many times to create an extremely rich sound. The 6th string has been dropped a whole step to D, which makes things sound even bigger. The intro runs a series of major triads over a pedal D bass before the main 9-bar rhythm figure is established at bar 8. Travis-style fingerpicking is used throughout this excerpt. Play the downstemmed notes with your thumb and the upstemmed part with your index finger. Lock onto this rhythm Figure (♪♫ ♫♪), memorize the chord forms, and you're on your way. You'll be ahead of the game when it comes to the upcoming tunes featuring Travis-picking.

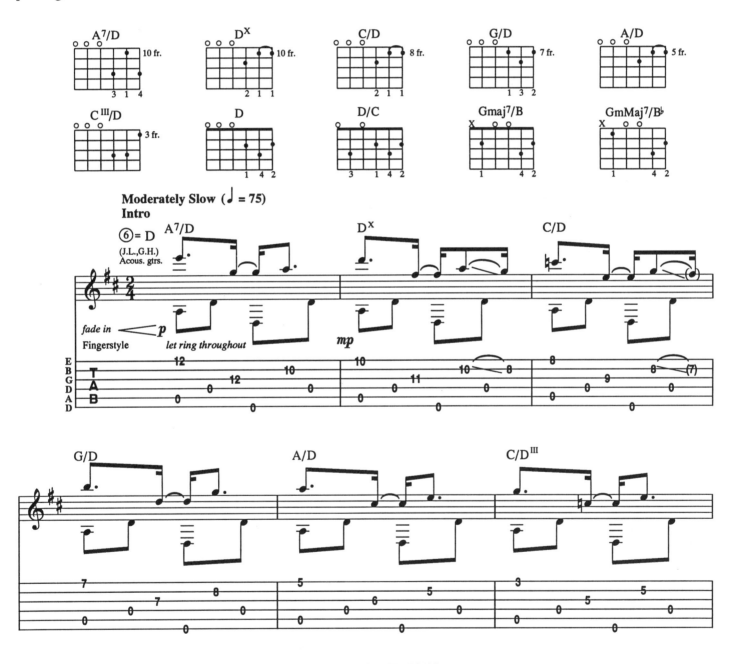

1st Verse
1. Dear Pru-dence

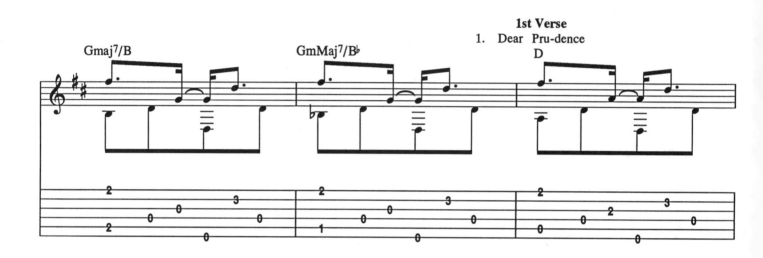

won't   you   come   out   to (play). `0:24`

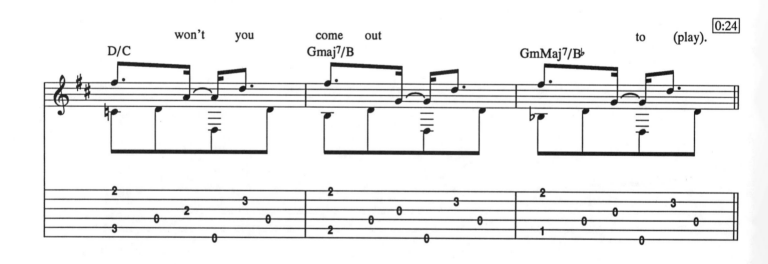

THE CONTINUING STORY OF BUNGALOW BILL

From the album *The Beatles*

Words and Music by John Lennon and Paul McCartney

Whether George, John or Paul actually played this Phrygian Spanish-style nylon-string intro is questionable. Perhaps it was a session musician or maybe it was even an early example of sampling off of one of the bands' favorite flamenco albums. Who knows? But one listen reveals some nice Em Phrygian-based runs that are worth checking out.

WHILE MY GUITAR GENTLY WEEPS

From the album *The Beatles*

Words and Music by George Harrison

Guest soloist, Eric Clapton, turns in a stellar performance on George's "While My Guitar Gently Weeps." His sweet tone and crying melodic phrases fit the song like a glove. E.C. explores the 12th position A pentatonic minor scale to the hilt before climbing to the 17th position for the climax. His sound may have been processed through a Leslie rotating speaker.

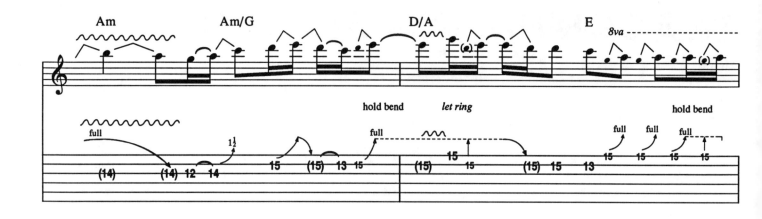

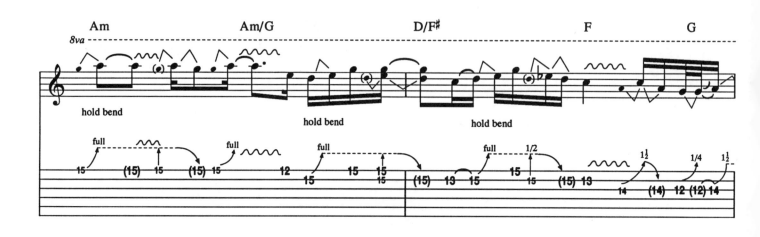

2:30 I don't know how...

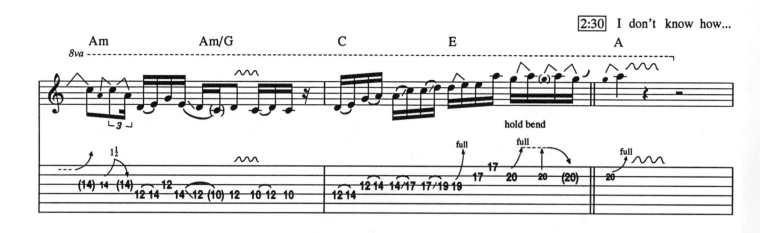

BLACKBIRD

From the album *The Beatles*
Words and Music by John Lennon and Paul McCartney

Paul's unique fingerpicking style produces many subtle variations. It's basically the same as Travis-style except the thumb and index finger brush one or more strings instead of plucking them dead on. Most of the chords are voiced on the 5th and 2nd strings against an open G pedal tone. Paul's voice leading is very smooth throughout the 3-bar intro and 18-bar verse.

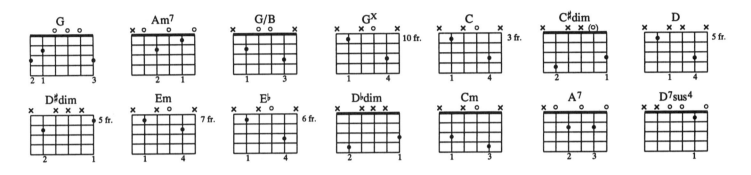

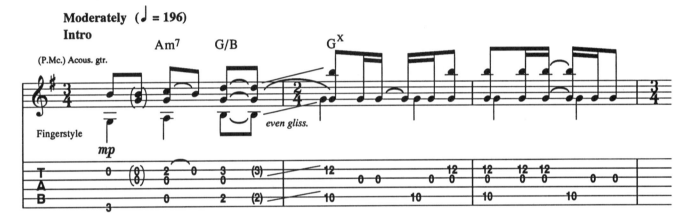

1st Verse

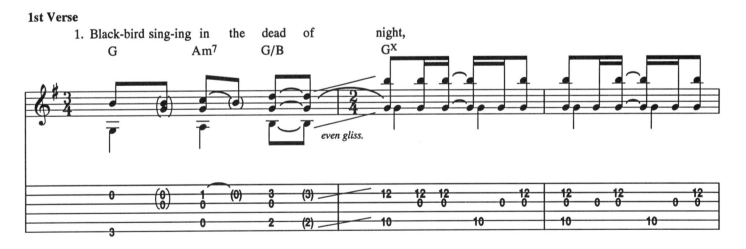

take these brok-en wings and learn to fly.

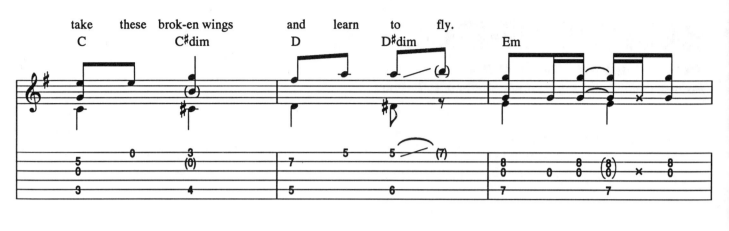

All your life,

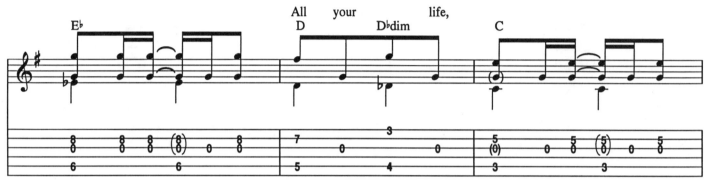

you were only wait-ing for this

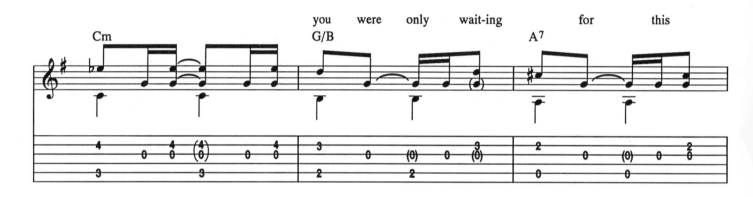

mo-ment to arise.

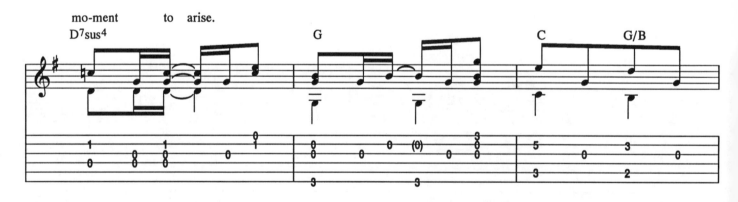

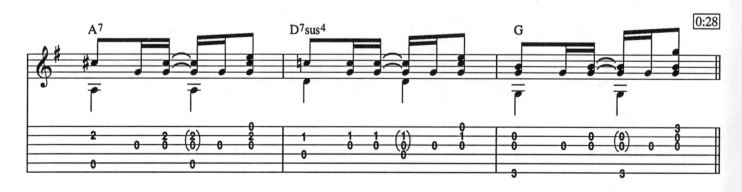

ROCKY RACCOON

From the album *The Beatles*
Words and Music by John Lennon and Paul McCartney

This folk ballad features an alternating bass/chord strum pattern by Paul. The 4-bar progression recycles throughout the song as he adds extensions and suspensions to the basic chord forms, with a swing-16th note feel.

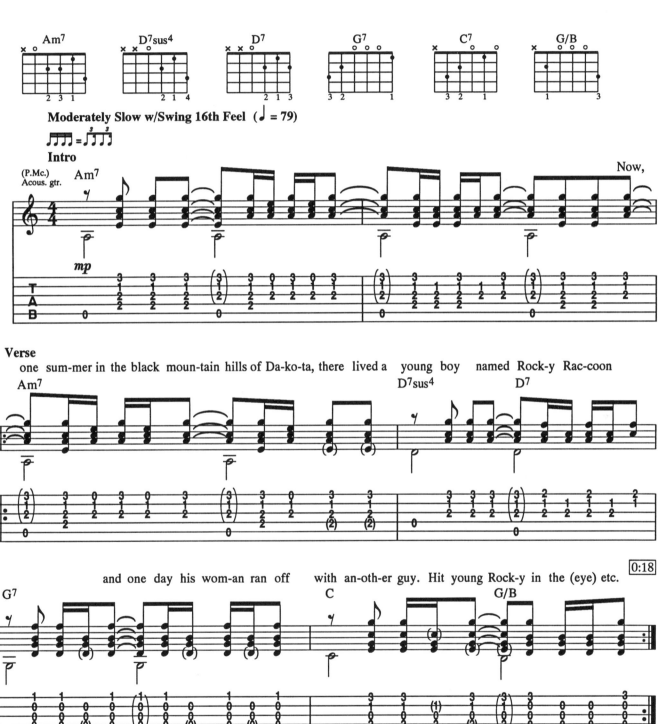

I WILL

From the album *The Beatles*
Words and Music by John Lennon and Paul McCartney

This almost-solo McCartney outing (Ringo played percussion) features a straight-8th 12-string acoustic rhythm figure punctuated by a heavily compressed 2-bar rockabilly-style signature riff in the 1st position. Note that only the first half of this riff is used in the transition the the B section. At 0:40, the 6-string acoustic plays a simple counterpoint line against the harmonized vocal melody, then restates half of the signature lick. The counterpoint line repeats but concludes this time with a descending series of 6ths played on the 1st and 3rd strings.

MCA music publishing

JULIA

From the album *The Beatles*
Words and Music by John Lennon and Paul McCartney

John's beautiful ballad features a double-tracked acoustic capoed at the 2nd fret. The Travis-style finger-picking is very similar to the pattern used on "Dear Prudence." Again, first memorize the overall rhythm figure, (♪♫ ♫♪) then learn the chord forms and apply the picking pattern to them. The thumb plays the downstemmed notes while the index finger plucks the upstemmed part.

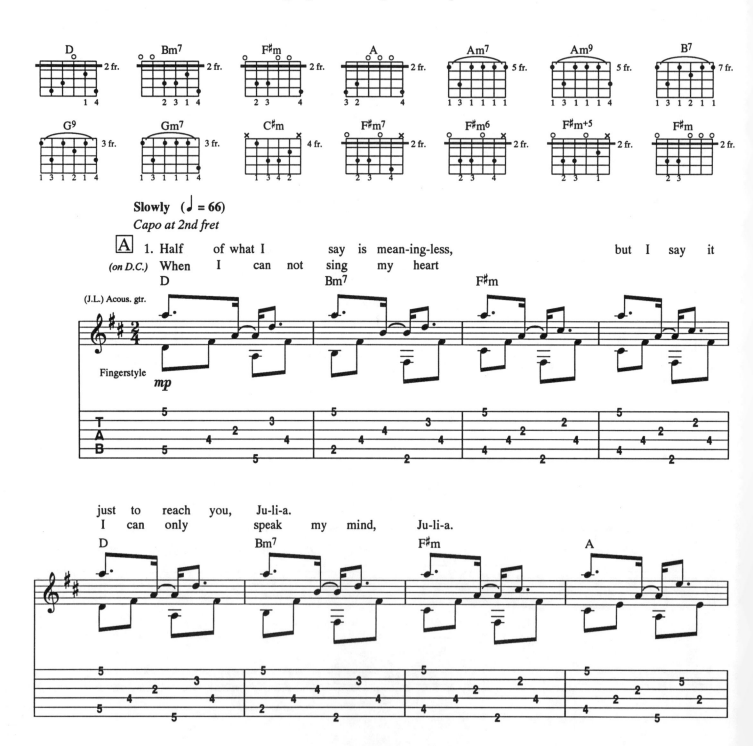

float-ing   sky,   is   shim-mer-ing,

glim-mer-ing   in   the   sun.

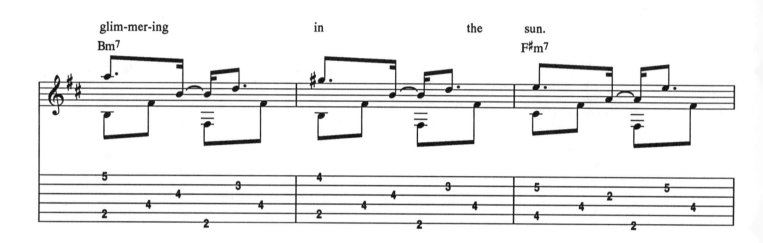

(Take 2nd ending)

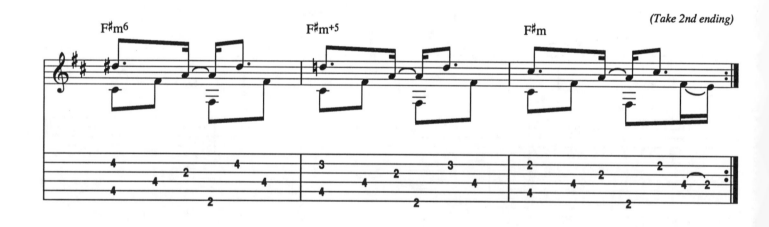

BIRTHDAY

From the album *The Beatles*

Words and Music by John Lennon and Paul McCartney

The main riff in this 12-bar rave up is played in octaves by George and John, though their parts are slightly different. George uses bends in the upper octave while John's part mixes doublestops with a single-note line. Paul doubles the main riff on bass but plays it straight through every bar instead of every other bar. Paul also doubles the cool interlude riff at 1:48.

1:48 **Interlude** (doubled by bass gtr.)

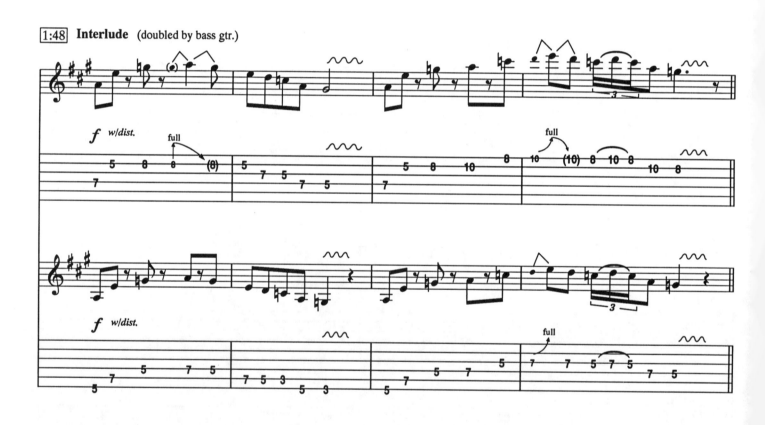

MOTHER NATURE'S SON

From the album *The Beatles*
Words and Music by John Lennon and Paul McCartney

Beginning at 2:15, Paul plays counterpoint against his verse rhythm figure while humming the melody. The rhythm figure features a swing-16th note feel except where even 16ths are indicated. The counterpoint moves from an arpeggiated suspension/resolution into unison with the melody before a descending 3rds harmony line concludes with a series of major triads over a pedal D.

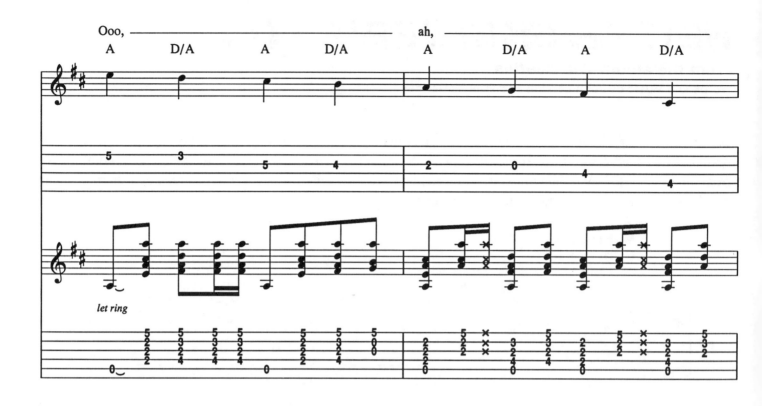

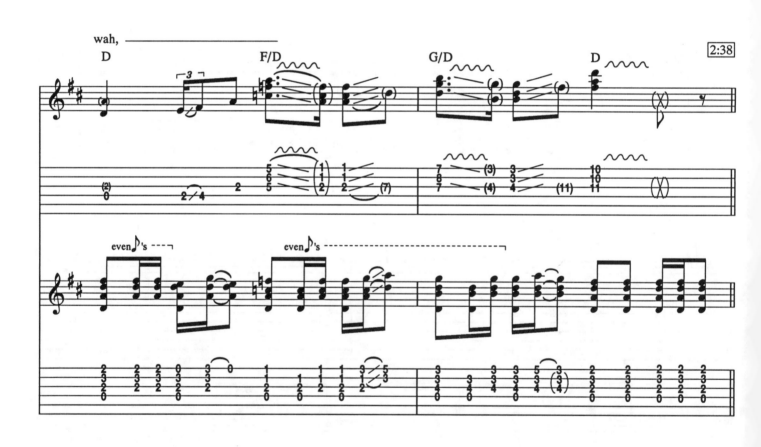

HELTER SKELTER

From the album *The Beatles*
Words and Music by John Lennon and Paul McCartney

The open 1st string provides an E pedal tone against a chromatically descending line on the B string for the intro to what is perhaps John Lennon's most raucous tune. The vocal melody moves in contrary motion as a false cadence to G drops to the tonic E for the cataclysmic rhythm figure. The guitars are being hit hard enough to knock the low E string slightly sharp with each attack. The chorus riff at 0:41 features call and response phrasing between the vocals and guitars. The IV chord (A) figure uses Root/5 and Root/6 chords followed by a rapid descending A mixolydian scale line. This figure is moved over one string group, which transposes it to E for the I chord. Another IV chord figure leads to the manic bend at the end of the chorus.

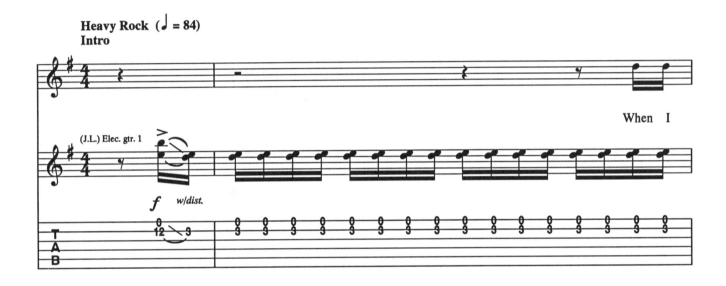

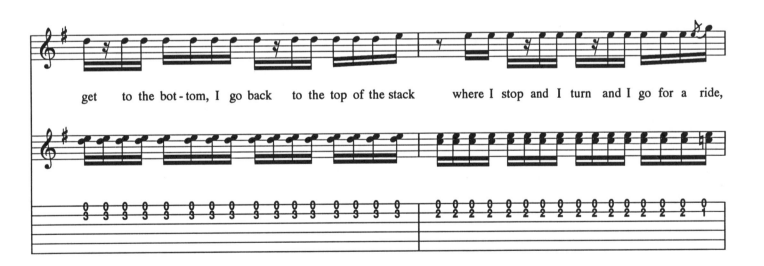

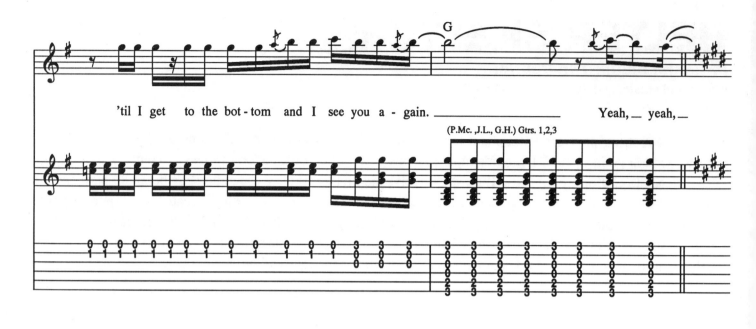

'til I get   to the bot-tom and I see you a-gain. _____   Yeah, _ yeah, _

(P.Mc. ,J.L., G.H.) Gtrs. 1,2,3

_ heh, heh, heh. _   Well,   do   you, don't   you want _ me to love _ you? _

0:41 **Chorus**

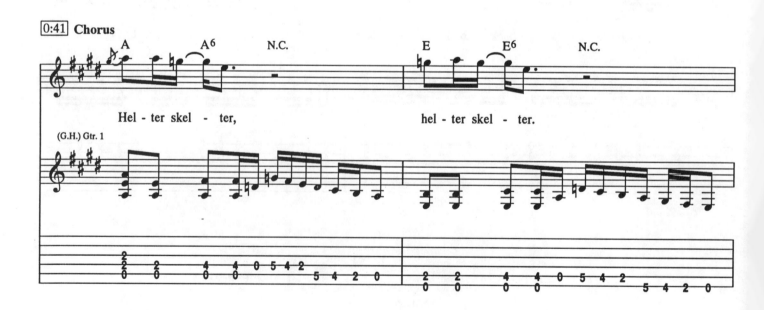

Hel - ter skel - ter,   hel - ter skel - ter.

(G.H.) Gtr. 1

ACROSS THE UNIVERSE

From the albums *Let It Be* and *Past Masters II*
Words and Music by John Lennon and Paul McCartney

Although John may be clearly seen rehearsing this song in the key of D in the Beatles' "Let It Be" film, it was eventually recorded in E♭. This intro excerpt is written in E♭ to be played with a capo at the 1st fret. You could also tune the entire guitar up 1/2 step and lower each fingering 1 fret. John begins with a series of 6th intervals over an E♭ pedal, then moves to a 3rd position Gm chord. He alternates the ♭3rd on the inside of the voicing with the 4th a whole step above. This gives a repeated suspension/resolution effect, and John continues this concept by adding the 9th to the following B♭ chord. Overall, he creates a lot of music in three bars. George's wah-wah subtly colors his unison part in bar 1; in bars 2 and 3, he articulates 16th notes with the pedal.

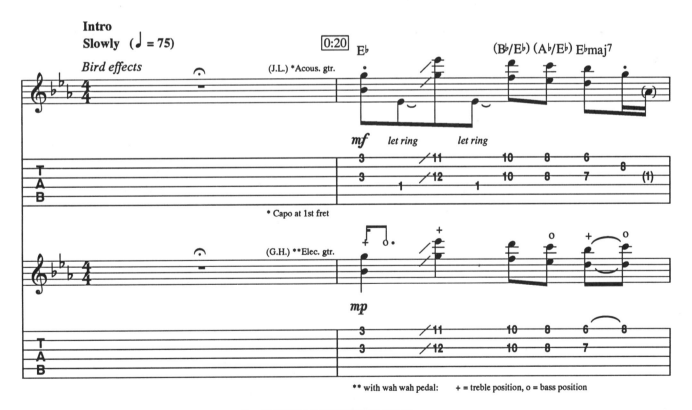

MCA music publishing

LET IT BE

From the album *Let It Be*

Words and Music by John Lennon and Paul McCartney

There are two different versions of George's "Let It Be" solo: one from the album, and one from the single. The album version solo features a second solo barely audible in the mix; this may have been an alternate take. All three solos feature a fat semi-distorted tone treated with a Leslie, and rely on the C pentatonic major scale for raw melodic material, although George plays each one differently.

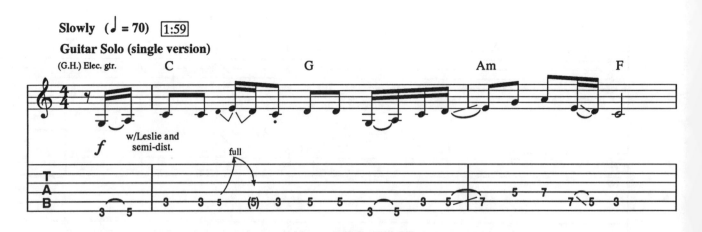

Let it be... 2.27 Chorus

LET IT BE (Album version)

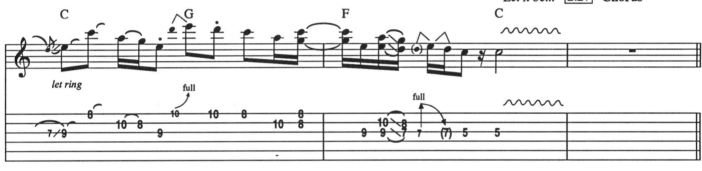

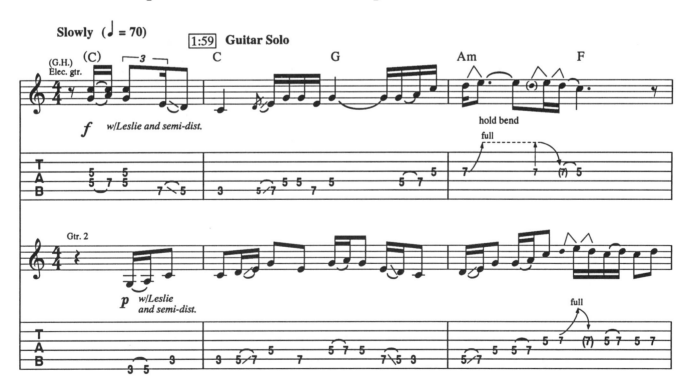

GET BACK

From the albums *Let It Be* and *Past Masters II*
Words and Music by John Lennon and Paul McCartney

George's muted rhythm figure lays down a solid pad for John's Chuck Berry-influenced pattern. Each vocal phrase lasts 3 bars and John answers on the 4th with a single-note riff in the 10th position. His chorus figure consists of a low register ascending pentatonic major lick followed by upper register 16th note flurries on the I7(A7) and IV7 (D7) chords. John's solo at [0:39] is a great example of call and response phrasing. A 2-bar lick in the 10th position is answered by a 2-bar response in the 7th and 5th positions. A variation of this 4-bar segment completes the 8-bar solo.

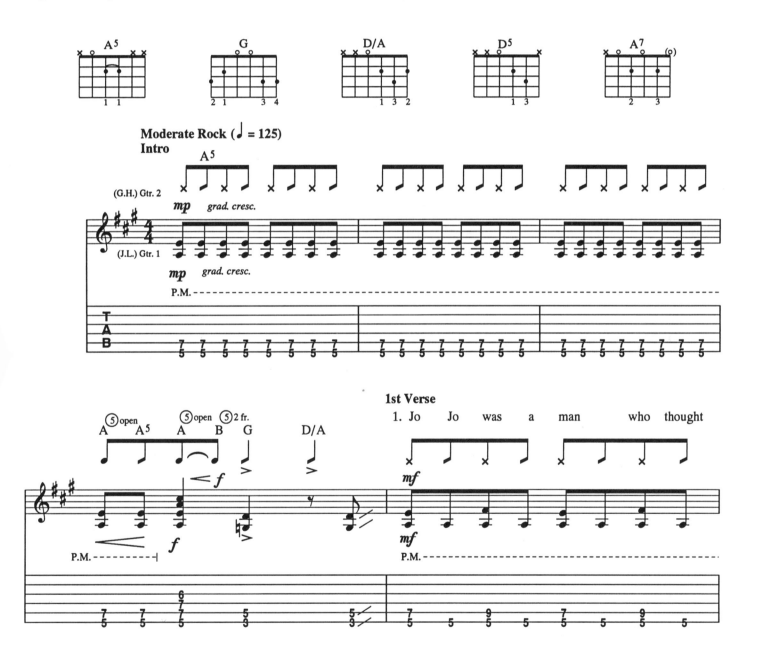

MCA music publishing

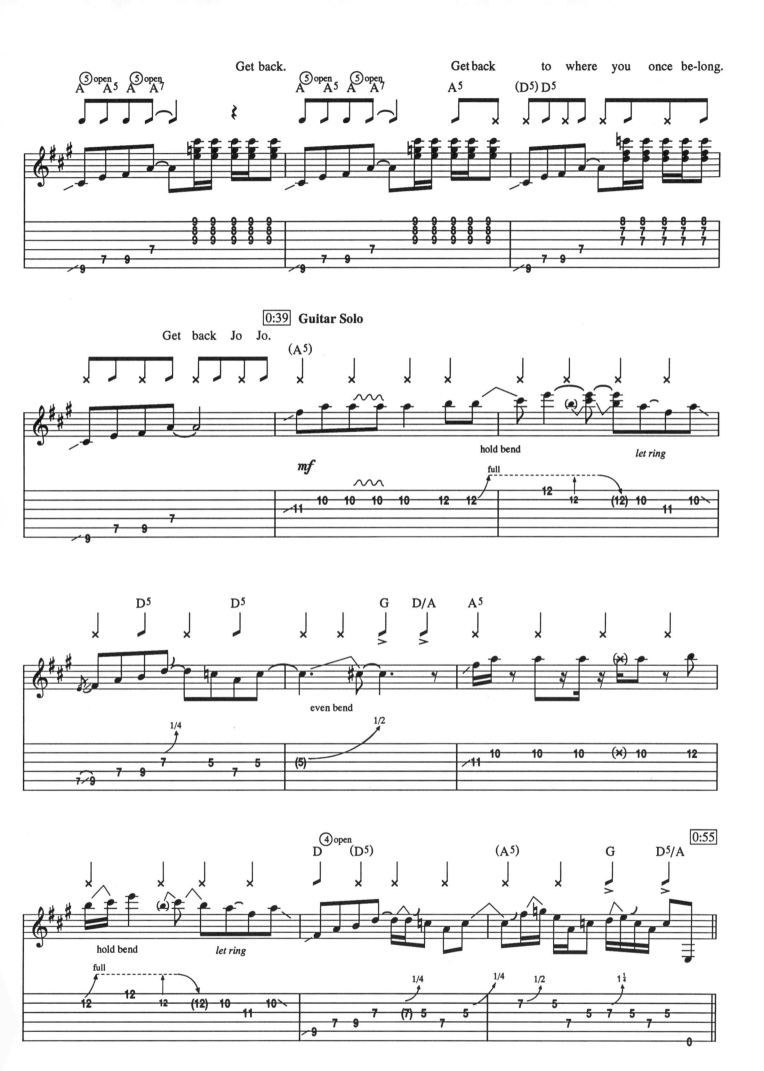

COME TOGETHER

From the album *Abbey Road*
Words and Music by John Lennon and Paul McCartney

This short Hendrix-flavored solo is harmonized in 4ths and 5ths. George's round, muted tone is produced by using the neck pickup with the tone control rolled back to the bass position in conjunction with a warm distorted basic sound. John semi-palm-mutes another Chuck Berry-style rhythm vamp underneath it all. The 4th verse excerpt is almost a slowed down version of "Memphis, Tennessee." George creates a sinister atmosphere using a volume pedal to swell into a close-voiced Dm7 while George and John quote the signature piano riff.

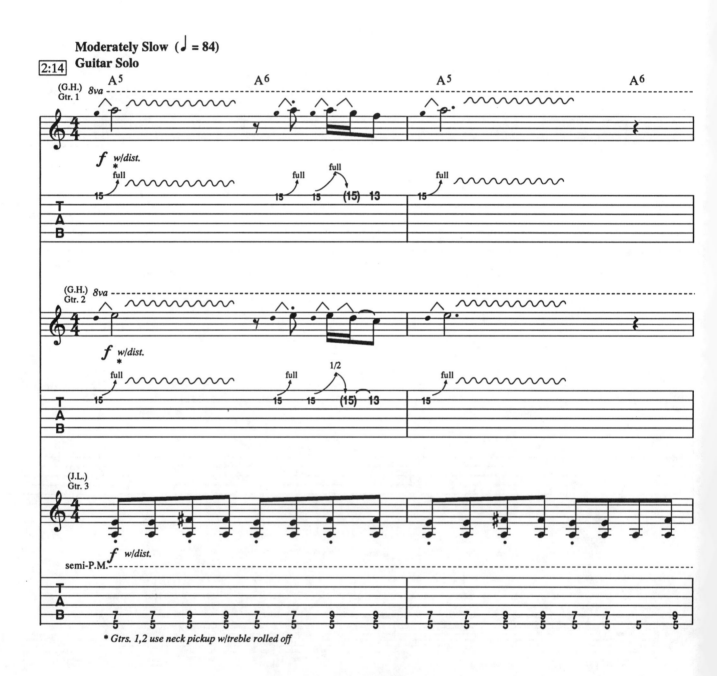

* Gtrs. 1,2 use neck pickup w/treble rolled off

MCA music publishing

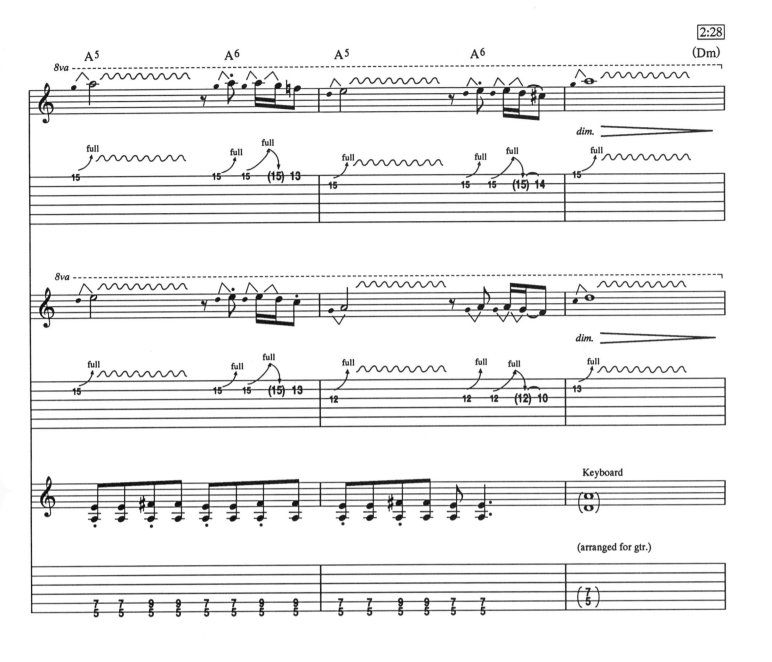

4th Verse

4. He roll-er coast-er, he got ear-ly warn-ing, he got

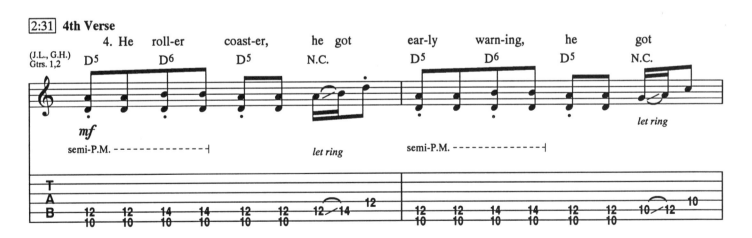

113

SOMETHING

From the album *Abbey Road*

Words and Music by George Harrison

This guitar solo stands as one of George's finest. Not one note is wasted as he plays through the 9-bar progression and develops a basic motif into an extremely memorable solo. George's Eric Clapton influences were never more present and his solo even rivals E.C.'s "While My Guitar Gently Weeps" in expression and melodic invention. The first 4 bars feature variations of the opening motif in the 12th position. In the following 2 measures, George's lines move lengthwise along the 4th, 2nd and 1st strings. A drop into the 5th position for some repeated melodic bends leads to a short stop at the 8th position before concluding with the song's signature lick in the 10th position.

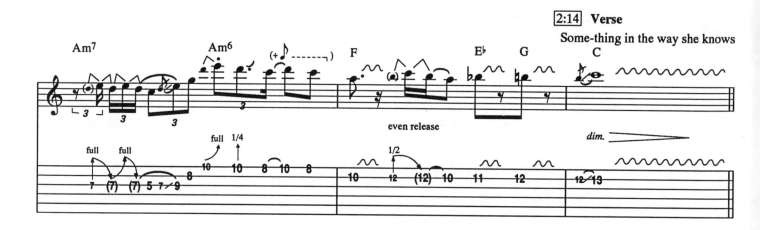

OH! DARLING

From the album *Abbey Road*

Words and Music by John Lennon and Paul McCartney

Paul's 50's-style ballad features George playing sharp backbeat chordal accents. Note the numerous slides following some of the attacks. In the B section, George arpeggiates upper register 4-note chord voicings with a staccato technique. His razor-treble tone was most likely produced by a Fender Telecaster. There's a very cool touch on the ending as George makes use of the short string length between the nut and turning pegs for some ethereal "string-pinging."

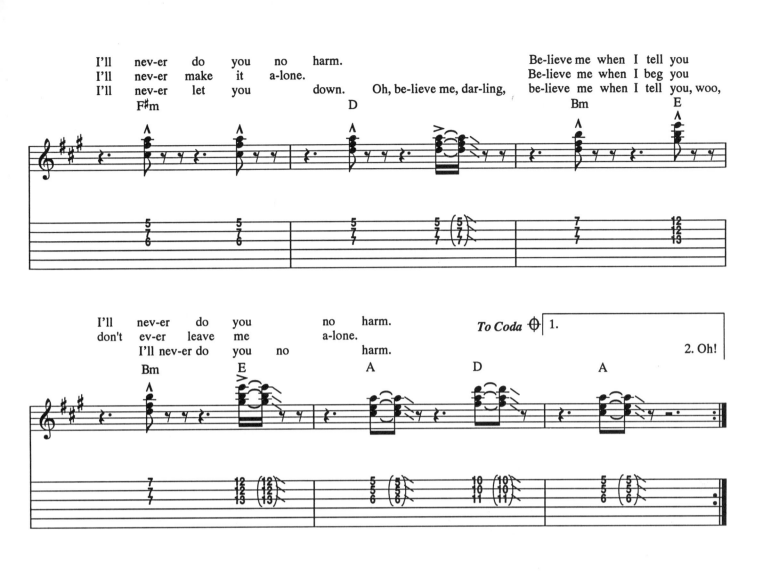

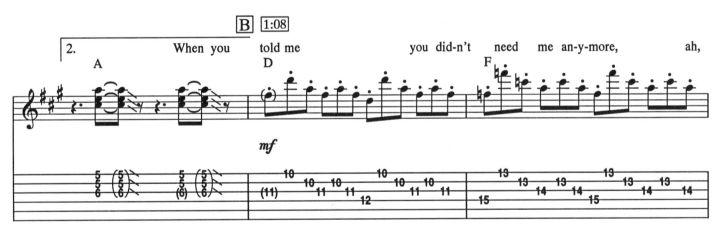

need me an-y-more,   ah, well you   know I   real-ly   broke   down   and died.   3. Oh,

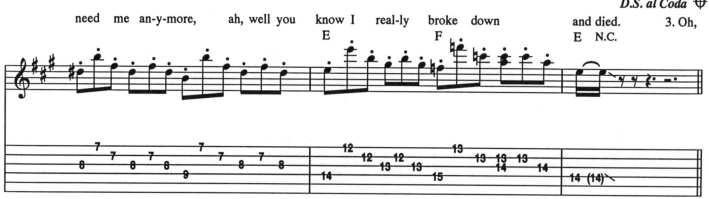

⊕ *Coda*

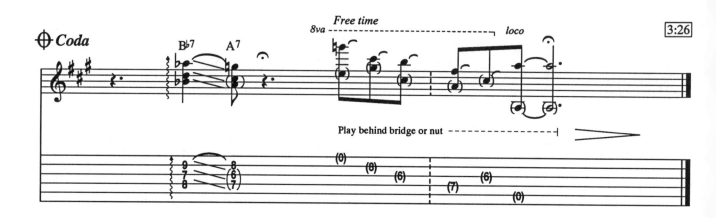

OCTOPUS'S GARDEN

From the album *Abbey Road*

Words and Music by Richard Starkey

George's 4-bar, country-style intro slides back and forth between the 9th and 12th positions before featuring a series of ascending chromatic 3rds and concluding with a drop into the 7th position. John's 2-bar rhythm figure outlines the I, vi, IV and V chords using Travis-style picking. The progression is elongated for the verse as each chord receives a full 4 beats. At 1:33 the figure modulates up a 4th to the key of A for George's 8-bar upper register solo drawing from A pentatonic major scale patterns in the 12th, 14th and 17th positions. John doubletimes the chords on the 7th bar, setting up a IV to V cadence back to the key of E.

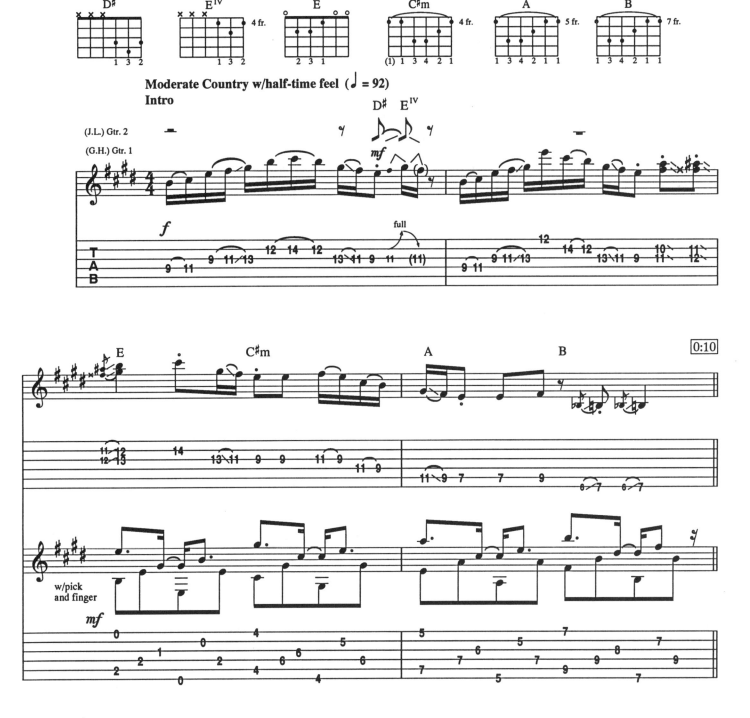

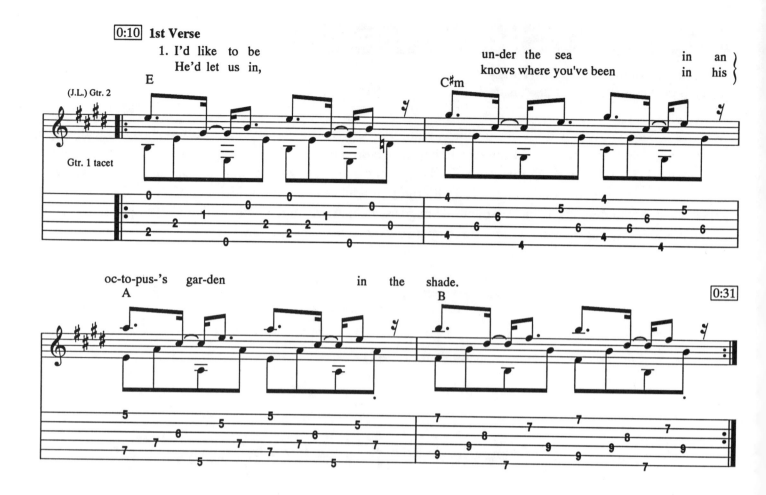

Octopus's Garden (Solo)

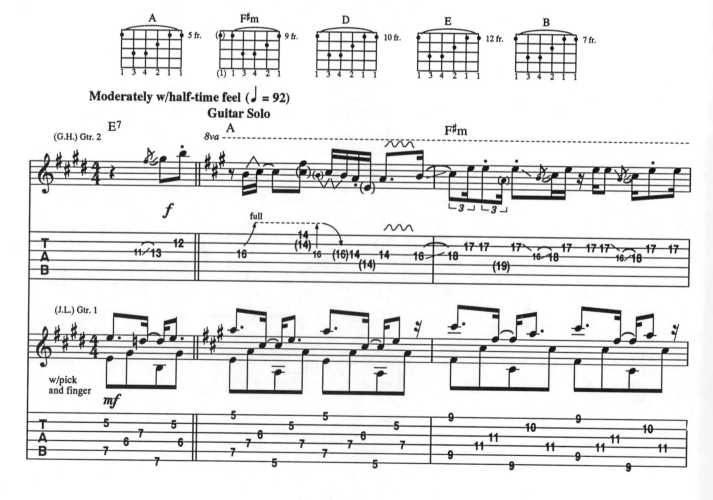

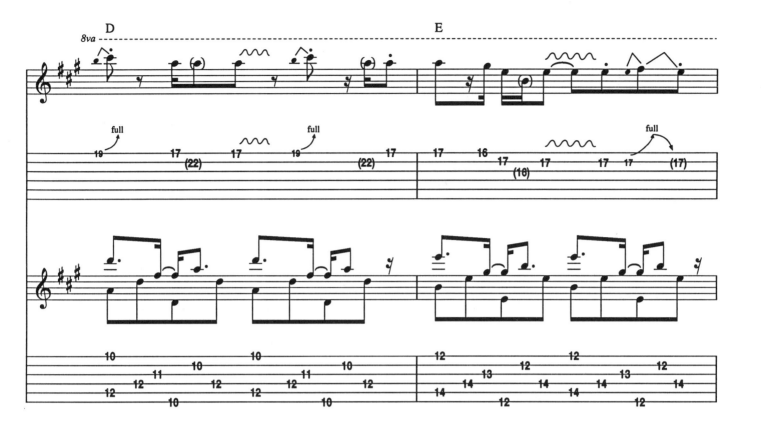

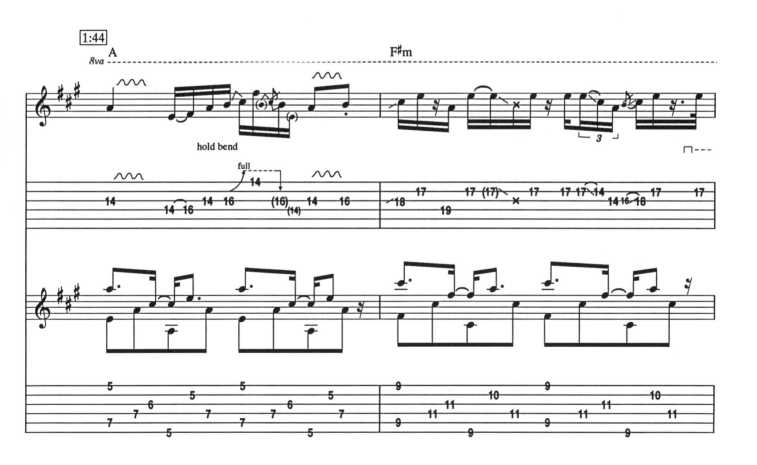

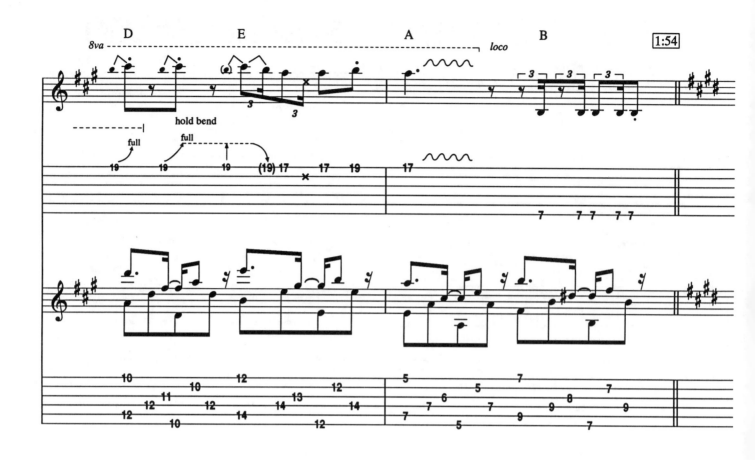

I WANT YOU (SHE'S SO HEAVY)

From the album *Abbey Road*
Words and Music by John Lennon and Paul McCartney

John and George created the massive guitar sound for the intro/chorus outro riff by tracking the part over and over. For the intro, John adds a brief solo, the ingenious open and 1st position signature rhythm figure, then segues into the song's jazzy 4/4 half-time verse groove. In bars 4-9, he plays along with his vocal lines while the rhythm section responds with short eighth note motifs in Am. Bars 10-14 conclude the Am section of the verse as the full band groove is established. Measures 15-22 are virtually the same as bars 4-11 transposed to D minor at the 10th position. This time the transitional 2/4 leads to 6 bars of altered V chord (E7♭9) accents framing Paul's famous bass breaks. A bar of silence punctuated by Ringo's hi-hat segues to the 2nd verse.

Beginning at 4:37, the final three minutes and two seconds feature a massive buildup of two simultaneous parts. The first reprises the intro and chorus chord riff while the second uses dropped D tuning to double the bass line. Instead of ending, the song simply stops abruptly in mid-phrase.

125

Total Heaviosity (♩. = 48)

(She's so...)

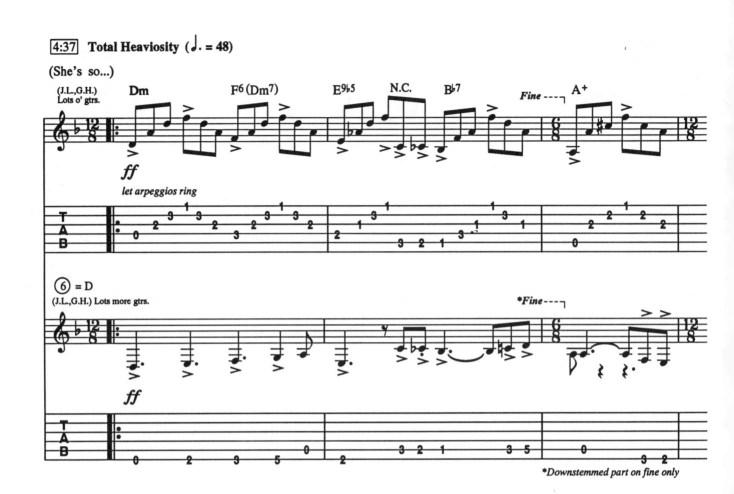

*Downstemmed part on fine only

126

BECAUSE

From the album *Abbey Road*
Words and Music by John Lennon and Paul McCartney

This beautiful 10-bar progression features uninterrupted eighth-note arpeggios which conceptually recall Beethoven's "Moonlight Sonata." The opening 4 bars of the intro are played by John on electric harpsichord. He doubles the part on electric guitar beginning at bar 5, continuing through the remainder of the progression and the repeat.

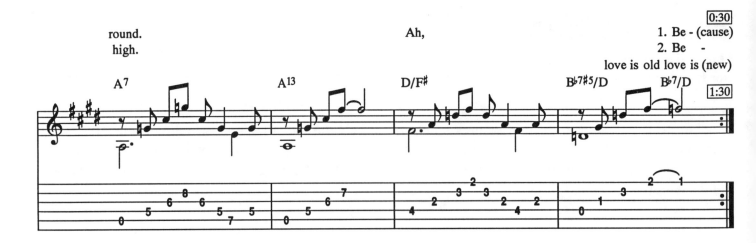

YOU NEVER GIVE ME YOUR MONEY

From the album *Abbey Road*

Words and Music by John Lennon and Paul McCartney

With enough different movements to qualify as a suite, this tune features an abundance of guitar work. At ⟨1:31⟩, George arpeggiates a classic 3-bar C Mixolydian chord progression (B♭, F, C) twice. John enters at ⟨1:48⟩, playing low register fills over background vocal "ah's" as George develops a 16th-note variation of the ♭VII, IV, I pattern and colors the F(IV) chord with a major 7th extension. At ⟨2:12⟩, both guitars begin a unison figure that spans the next 6 bars and features a diminished lick ascending in minor 3rds, climaxing with a series of chromatic 6ths. The modulation at ⟨2:28⟩ introduces a new vocal against George's fuzzy 4-bar Chuck Berry-style vamp while John fills underneath. The mood switches for two bars of a D Dorian progression which results from moving F, G and Am triads over a pedal D bass note. A 1 1/2 bar restatement of the melody segues to the classic arpeggiateed C, G/B to A progression, enhanced by George's shimmering Leslie-treated sound.

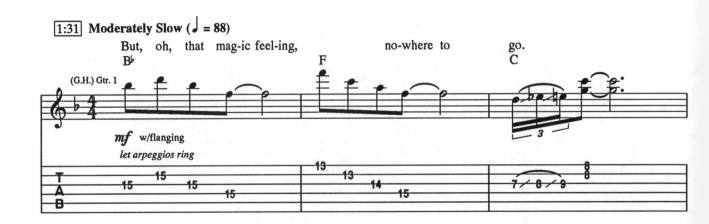

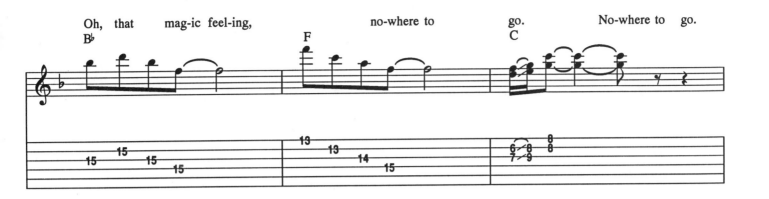

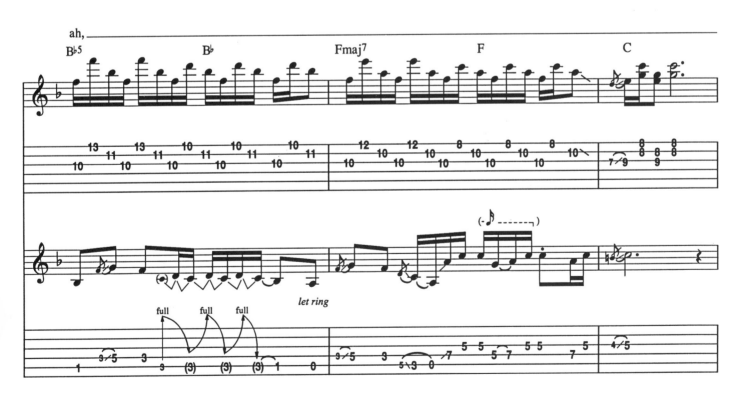

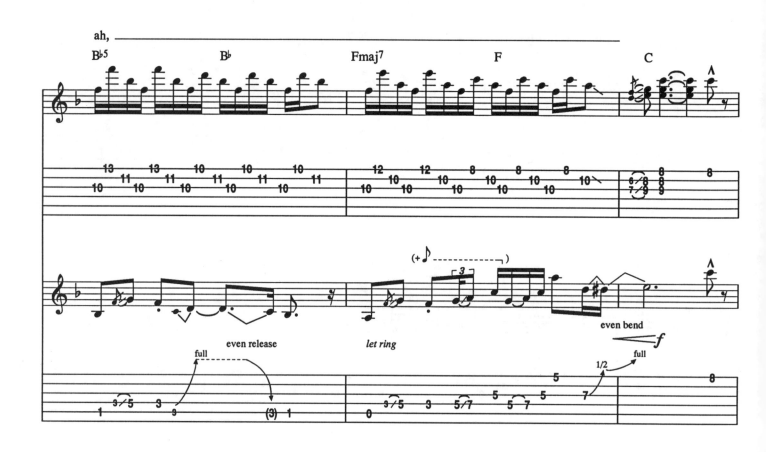

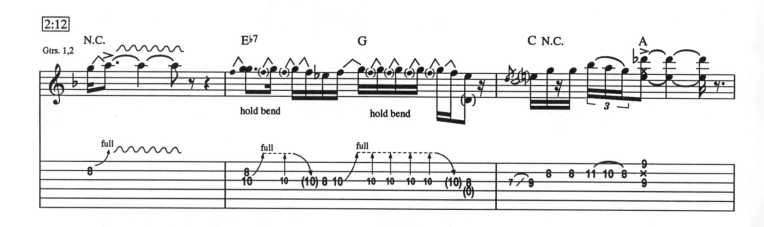

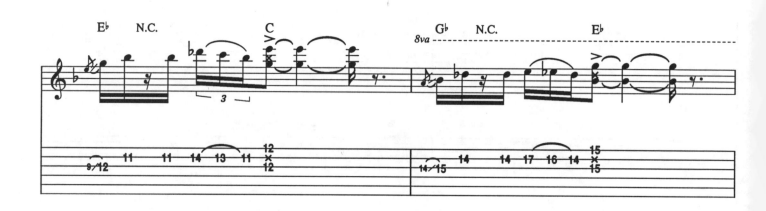

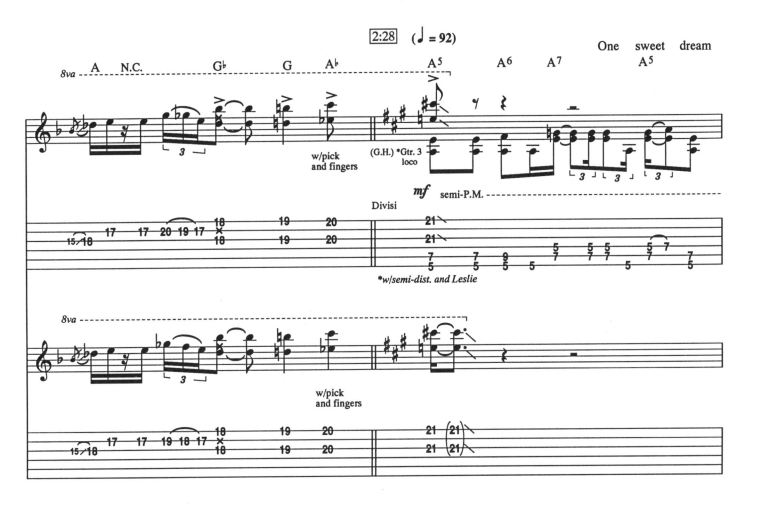

One sweet dream

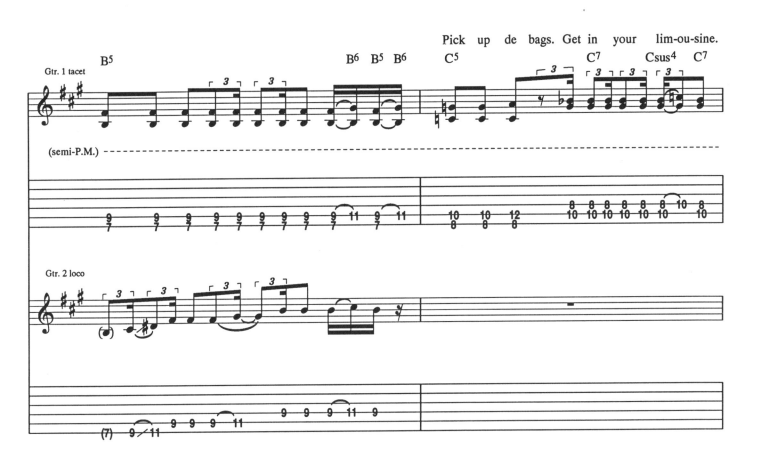

Pick up de bags. Get in your lim-ou-sine.

131

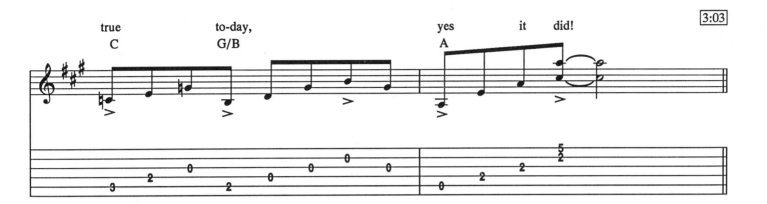

SUN KING

From the album *Abbey Road*

Words and Music by John Lennon and Paul McCartney

Described by George as the Beatles' attempt to be Fleetwood Mac doing "Albatross," this lush ballad creates some lovely imagery. His bass register signature line is treated with amp tremolo and reverb. John enters at bar 5 with a Travis-picked figure using A6, B6 and E6. Adding 6ths to the I, IV and V triads gives them a dreamy quality. At bar 13, he switches to a chord melody approach using A#6 as a chromatic passing chord between A6 and B6. The modulation to C for the verse concludes this excerpt.

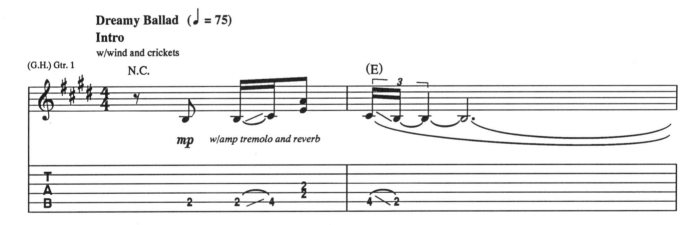

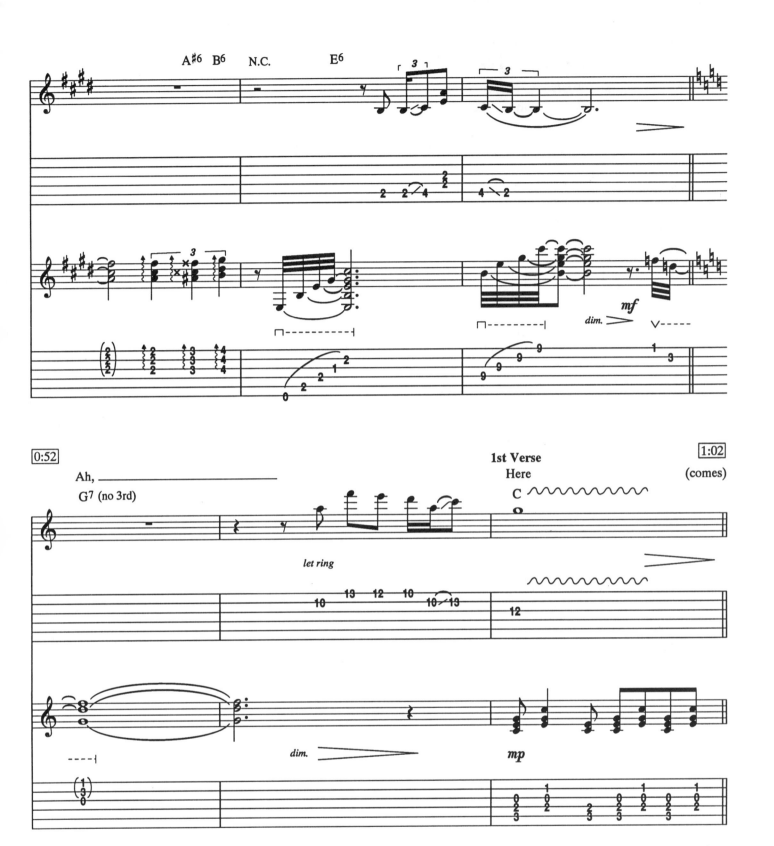

POLYTHENE PAM

From the album *Abbey Road*
Words and Music by John Lennon and Paul McCartney

It's unclear who the soloist is on this tune. The unorthodox fingerings suggest it was Paul, but it could have been George or John as well. John wrote the song and definitely played the classic 3-chord 12-string part. He makes ample use of the open G6 all-purpose passing chord throughout the solo. What sounds like the end of the solo is actually the intro to Paul's "She Came In Through The Bathroom Window." Both songs were recorded as one, another Beatle first.

("She Came in Through the Bathroom Window" Intro)

THE END

From the album *Abbey Road*
Words and Music by John Lennon and Paul McCartney

The running order of soloists is clear: all three guitarists trade 2-bar phrases with Paul kicking off, followed by George and John. They are all in top form and this excellent solo provides a great opportunity to examine each Beatles' lead guitar style.

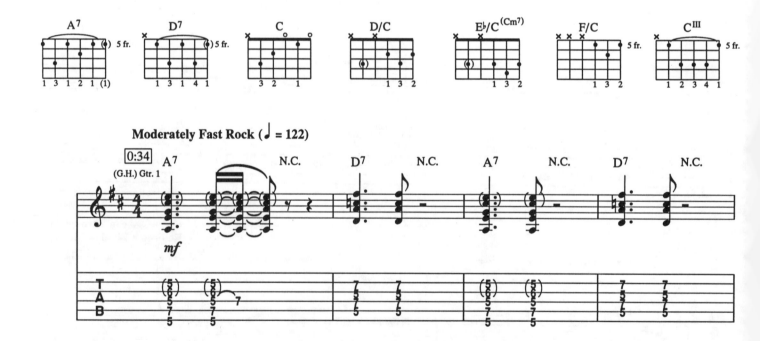

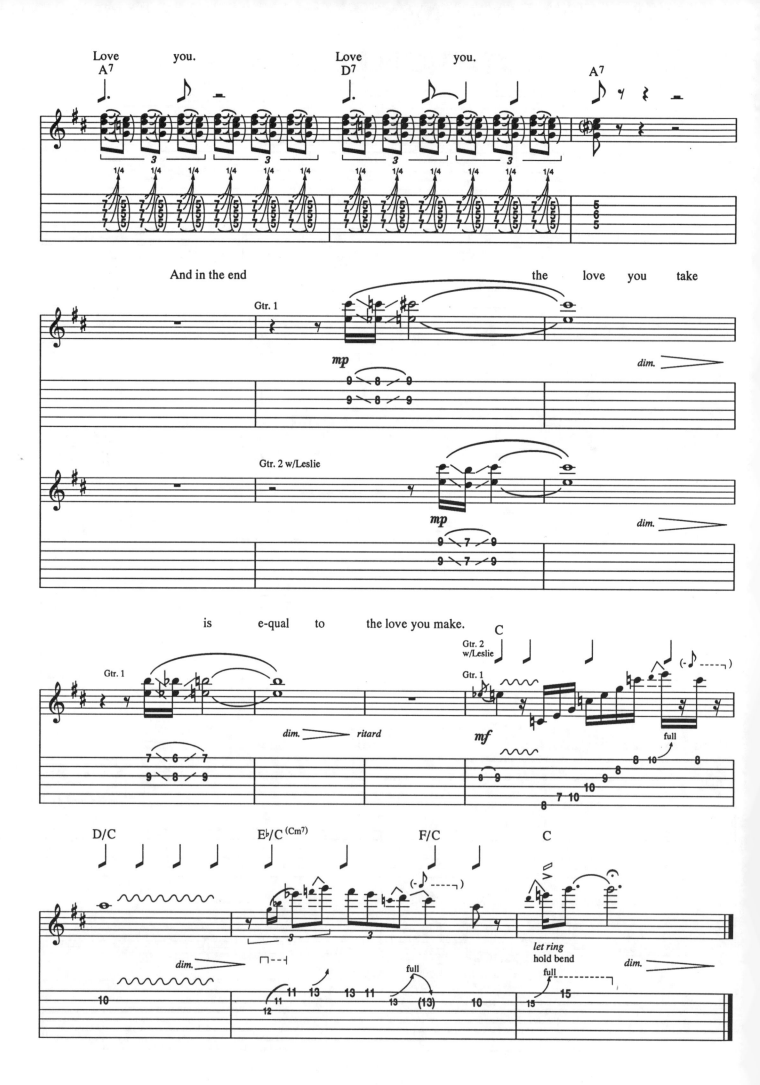